12/04

UNIVERSITY OF
WOLVERHAMPTON ·
ENTERPRISE LTD.

Harrison Learning Centre
Wolverhampton Campus
University of Wolverhampton
St Peter's Square
Wolverhampton WV1 1RH
Wolverhampton (01902) 322305

THE BUSINESS OF
CHILDREN'S ENTERTAINMENT

THE GUILFORD COMMUNICATION SERIES

Editors

Theodore L. Glasser, Stanford University

Marshall S. Poole, Texas A & M University

Advisory Board

Charles Berger	Peter Monge	Michael Schudson
James W. Carey	Barbara O'Keefe	Linda Steiner

Recent Volumes

THE BUSINESS OF CHILDREN'S ENTERTAINMENT
Norma Odom Pecora

CASE STUDIES IN ORGANIZATIONAL COMMUNICATION 2:
PERSPECTIVES ON CONTEMPORARY WORK LIFE
Beverly Davenport Sypher, *Editor*

REGULATING MEDIA: THE LICENSING AND SUPERVISION OF
BROADCASTING IN SIX COUNTRIES
Wolfgang Hoffman-Riem

COMMUNICATION THEORY: EPISTEMOLOGICAL FOUNDATIONS
James A. Anderson

TELEVISION AND THE REMOTE CONTROL: GRAZING ON A
VAST WASTELAND
Robert V. Bellamy, Jr., and James R. Walker

RELATING: DIALOGUES AND DIALECTICS
Leslie A. Baxter and Barbara M. Montgomery

DOING PUBLIC JOURNALISM
Arthur Charity

SOCIAL APPROACHES TO COMMUNCIATION
Wendy Leeds-Hurwitz, *Editor*

PUBLIC OPINION AND THE COMMUNICATION OF CONSENT
Theodore L. Glasser and Charles T. Salmon, *Editors*

COMMUNICATION RESEARCH METHODS: A SOURCEBOOK
Rebecca B. Rubin, Philip Palmgreen, and Howard E. Sypher, *Editors*

PERSUASIVE COMMUNICATION
James B. Stiff

REFORMING LIBEL LAW
John Soloski and Randall P. Bezanson, *Editors*

MESSAGE EFFECTS RESEARCH: PRINCIPLES OF DESIGN AND
ANALYSIS
Sally Jackson

CRITICAL PERSPECTIVES ON MEDIA AND SOCIETY
Robert K. Avery and David Eason, *Editors*

The Business of Children's Entertainment

NORMA ODOM PECORA

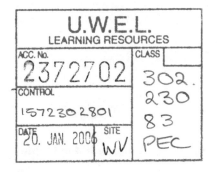
THE GUILFORD PRESS
New York   London

© 1998 Norma Odom Pecora
Published by The Guilford Press
A Division of Guilford Publications, Inc.
72 Spring Street, New York, NY 10012
www.guilford.com

Printed in the United States of America

This book is printed on acid-free paper.

Last digit is print number: 9 8 7 6 5 4 3 2 1

Library of Congress Cataloging-in-Publication Data

Pecora, Norma Odom. The business of children's entertainment / Norma Odom Pecora.
        p.   cm.–(The Guilford communication series)
    Includes bibliographical references and index.
    ISBN 1-57230-280-1
    1. Advertising–Children's paraphernalia.
    2. Child consumers. 3. Television advertising and children.
    4. Motion pictures and children. 5. Toy industry. 6. Children's clothing industry. 7. TV and movie tie-ins. I. Series.
    HF6161.C33P43   1998
    658.8′34′083–dc21   97–40876
                                                                CIP

Acknowledgments

Like all authors, I owe a number of professional and personal debts. While writing Chapter 2, I was supported by a grant from the National Endowment for the Humanities, Summer Stipend Program. In addition, two anonymous reviewers helped me rethink and clarify ideas and thoughts, as have many students along the way. Ellen Wartella and Sharyne Merritt taught me the skills necessary to assume this task, and as Editor, Peter Wissoker has been an encouraging voice.

Personal debts are incalculable. To sisters who are always there; to Jay and Sarah, who started me down this road; and to a partner's great patience—thank you all.

Contents

THE BUSINESS OF CHILDREN'S ENTERTAINMENT

Introduction

> Culture may be defined as the whole
> body of beliefs, practices and material
> artifacts that a society uses. Our culture
> is commercial because of the central
> place material goods and reminders of
> material goods have in it. But the term
> "commercial culture" can be used in
> another sense as well, when applied to
> the flow of ideas and expressions that
> shape our national character and
> outlook.
>
> —BOGART (1991, p. 2)

Not long ago, while out shopping, I saw a little girl of 5 dressed in a Minnie and Me T-shirt and matching shorts, with the Little Mermaid on her tennis shoes, and a My Little Pony in her hand. Ah ha, I thought—a child of her culture.

Until recently, discussions of "commercial culture" have excluded children. As a result, with a few exceptions, little thought has been given to the *economic forces* that shape their culture even though the artifacts and conversations of children now reflect a world of material possessions (for exceptions see Englehardt, 1987; McNeal, 1987, 1992; Luke, 1990; Seiter, 1993; Kline, 1993). This book will examine children's

1

culture in the context of the economic decisions that have driven the children's entertainment business and consequently shaped that culture.

It is difficult to capture a single point in time when writing a book like this: Today's Power Rangers are next week's Teenage Mutant Ninja Turtles. When this idea began in the early 1980s, the three television networks dominated children's entertainment; as the book goes to press, new distribution outlets are announced almost daily. There are venues such as CDs and computer games that were not even thought of as family entertainment in the early 1980s. Consequently, this is not an attempt to predict a future landscape; rather, its intent is to present a theoretical model to describe and explain that landscape, whatever it may be. Therefore, this book sets out to accomplish two goals:

1. To describe the children's entertainment industry at one point in time.
2. To introduce a model that serves to explain how decisions were made in the industries involved.

The theoretical model of political economy will be used to explore the structure and connections that brought about the current landscape. By acknowledging that the media industries in the United States are profit-driven, commercial organizations, the intersection between commerce and entertainment become apparent and future changes will be better understood.

This analysis begins with the caveat that the ideological dimension should not be ignored; however, this dimension and the significance of the idea that "the flow of ideas and expressions shape our national character and outlook," has been addressed elsewhere (Luke, 1990; Seiter, 1993; Kline, 1994). Therefore the primary focus here will be on the *how* and *why* of Minnie and Me T-shirts and Little Mermaid tennis shoes, the *material goods*, not the cultural implications. Central to the analysis is the recognition that entertainment industries, like all commercial industries, strive to maintain and maximize profits within the context of social, political, and economic constraints. Such constraints shaped, and continue to shape, children's entertainment.

Television has been described as a business that works on three simple principles:

> Keep the audience up,
> keep the costs down,
> keep the regulators out. (Schneider, 1987, p. 5)

To this the children's television industry has added a fourth: Find someone else to pay the bills. This is the story of how the toy industry came to be that "someone else." Toy companies and the children's entertainment industry have long had a casual working relationship. After all, the movies brought us Shirley Temple dolls. However, over time this relationship has changed from simple, contractual agreements to more complex arrangements. Economic factors have been at the center of these changes, and their consequences are the focus here—how two industries, the toy industry and the television industry, came to redefine children's entertainment.

A FRAMEWORK FOR ANALYSIS

Previous work in political economy presents a direction for analyzing the structure of children's entertainment. Therefore, this analysis begins with the recognition that the mass media are "first and foremost industrial and commercial organizations which produce and distribute commodities" (Murdock & Golding, 1974, p. 205). One cannot deny that the media industries have an ideological component—they are our contemporary storytellers—but here, the economic framework is brought to the foreground.

Central to this understanding is the recognition that the children's toy and media industries, like all commercial industries, need to maintain and maximize profits, but they must work within the context of social, political, and economic constraints. For example, during the 1970s and early 1980s, a set of events altered previous arrangements between the toy and television industries. A shrinking supply of programs and advertising time, an increasing population of children, the deregulation of the television industry, and a growing toy industry all came together to reshape children's media.

This book will provide an analytical framework to explain these changes: how attempts to spread economic risk and assure profitability combined with increasing economic concentration and consolidation of the industries led to particular consequences.

To view media as the output of a commercial system does not preclude the consideration of an ideological force; rather, it adds a further dimension to the discussion. The media are viewed as a complex process with, in this case, economic influences as central.

Our starting point will be the commodity—the child as consumer and as audience.

Some of the issues considered in analyzing the material world of childhood include the growth of the child-as-consumer (Chapter 1) and as-audience (Chapter 2), the structure of children's entertainment and toy industries (Chapter 3), programs and products that demonstrate changes in the market (Chapter 4), new alliances that continue the consumer-oriented trends (Chapters 5 and 6), and the expansion into the international marketplace (Chapter 7). Finally, the consequences of these changes will be considered.

Before beginning, it is important to clarify three terms. First, *children* and *youth* are generic terms used here to mean children under the age of 13; the terms are used interchangeably. Adolescents, tweens (9–12) and teenagers (13+), will be included on occasion but generally identified as such. When speaking of children as consumer or audience, this book speaks of all children regardless of gender, race, or ethnicity. It can be argued that some children, like some adults, have more "value" than others because of their gender or economic status. This book does not make that distinction. Most children go to the store; most children watch television; and all children are exposed to the culture described here.

Second, the book concentrates on the *product manufacturing industries* relevant to children. Product manufacturers are those industries that generate consumer goods and services such as toys, food, and clothing; however, fast-food restaurants are included because they advertise heavily to children contributing to this culture. In addition, the restaurants are also important, because they frequently conduct advertising campaigns linked with media events. Advertisers will be seen as the voice of these industries.

Finally, because this discussion cannot be limited to television, the term *entertainment industry* will be used when referencing the range of media products available to the child—books, radio, records, motion pictures, videocassettes, audiocassettes, video games, and computer software. Along the way, the impact of government regulation and character licensing on these media markets will also be examined, because both contribute to the understanding of the business of children's entertainment.

As with any assessment of "things present," there must be an understanding of "things past," so the book begins with a history of children as consumers and as audience. However, although historical in scope, the book will pivot on the 1970s and early 1980s, when the link between product and programming gained attention. Where once there were shelves of generic toys such as teddy bears, trucks, and dolls, with the 1980s came thousands of merchandise items selling Strawberry Shortcake, the Smurfs, He-Man, and G.I. Joe—all for sale and for entertainment.

1
♦♦♦

Children Become Consumers

In recent years, charges have been leveled at the children's entertainment industry claiming that cartoon characters are nothing more than hucksters for a variety of merchandise to be sold to children. Clothing apparel, vitamins, and breakfast cereals designed specifically for the child are sold by a multitude of anthropomorphic animals and cartoon characters. This chapter offers an explanation of how this phenomenon, teddy bear as huckster, has come about by examining the role of children in a market economy. It is the story of how children came to be defined as consumers and the way that plays into the business of children's entertainment.

Others have identified childhood as a social and cultural concept (see, e.g., Elkind, 1981; Winn, 1984; Meyrowitz, 1985; Postman, 1985; Holland, 1992); however, *childhood* is also an economic construct (Zelizer, 1985). When labor is in short supply, for instance, families are large; children are useful as active participants on farms or in labor-intensive industries. And when, as in advanced capitalism, there is a need for markets to consume goods and services, children become valuable as consumers.

Children must be recognized as consumers before their importance as "audience" can be understood, for central to the growth of a child audience is the concept of the child-market. The characteristics of any market are the size of the group, its ability to buy, a desire or need for a product, the authority to purchase a specific product, an understanding of money, and a willingness to part with their money (McNeal, cited in Summers, 1971; Pride & Ferrel, cited in McNeal, 1987). Once children, as a group, met these qualifications, they became a "market," and it became practical to advertise to them.

Corporate America, in the form of advertisers and product manufacturers, and the children's entertainment industry have long had a casual working relationship. However, over time, this relationship has changed from simple, contractual agreements between the entertainment and manufacturing industries to more complex economic arrangements. Entertainment characters now not only sell goods but also are part and parcel of the product. No longer does Johnny ask mom to buy Ovaltine drink because Little Orphan Annie or Dick Tracy say so; now Johnny wants Batman cereal, a Looney Tunes frozen dinner, Sesame Street pasta shapes, or Smurf yogurt. The entertainment personality becomes the brand name.

Several factors that have contributed to this shift, beginning with the socialization and definition of children as consumers, will be developed here. Children are "trained to fit cultural role systems which will presumably exist when they are adults" (Mayer, Zussman, & Stamp, 1979); they are socialized for the role of consumer. As children gain access to spending money, they become valued as consumers. From 1900 to 1940, children were seen primarily as influencing family purchases or being encouraged to spend their own money wisely. With the expanding economy of the 1950s, and the baby boom, "teenagers" came to be defined as a consumer market. By 1980, children as young as age 5 were encouraged to think "brand label." The 1990s brought consumer outlets that were previously adult oriented but are now designed specifically for children—Walden Kids, GapKids, and Talbots Kids and Babies.

This evolution reflects three historical phases of a consumer market:

> Phase I, fragmentation . . . small producers sell low-volume output at high margins to restricted market . . . geographic segmentation . . . [in]adequate transportation and communication infrastructures.
>
> Phase II, unification . . . marked by the development, promotion, and exploitation of mass markets.
>
> Phase III, segmentation . . . specialized outputs that catered to demographic and psychographic consumer segments. (Tedlow, cited in Hollander & Germain, 1992, pp. 1–2)

Phase I occurred in the United States during the preindustrial period ending about the late 1800s; Phase II reflects the early days of promoting the consumption of mass produced goods and still occurs each time a new medium is introduced (see, e.g., Ewen, 1988, or Strasser, 1989). As markets in the United States move into Phase III, children, like adults, become a specialized market to be identified and courted. In addition to having their own money, there are a number of reasons advertisers pursue children: because they influence family purchases ("Sell the Kids," 1965; McNeal, 1992a, 1992b); to help them develop money-management skills (Gruenberg & Gruenberg, 1931); to train them to be consumers (Reisman, Glaser, & Revel, 1979); to make a variety of programming available (Association of National Advertisers, 1978); and to expand the market potential for goods (Gilbert, 1957). Children are a current market, a future market, and an influential market (McNeal, 1987).

HISTORY OF MARKETING TO CHILDREN

The earliest marketing to children developed at the turn of the century, when food and household-product companies used trade cards, storybooks, and dolls such as the Campbell

Kids as entertainment and advertisement (Strasser, 1989; Formanek-Brunell, 1993).[1] With the introduction of radio, a medium that relied on selling commercial airtime, advertisers turned to radio to reach audiences of consumers. During the first decade of radio, advertisers continued the merchandising of household products to children. Program or advertising time was sold to food companies such as General Foods and Wrigley Chewing Gum. With television, new products entered the arena. Toy companies realized the advantage of this exciting visual medium to demonstrate the abilities of their products. Events such as Mattel's entrance into the program production arena, first in 1969 with *Hot Wheels,* an animated program based on a line of their toy cars, and later in 1983 with *He-Man and the Masters of the Universe,* action figures that were also a syndicated cartoon program, did not occur without precedent. They are the direct consequence of the definition of children as consumer market and as audience commodities.

1930 to 1940

Early radio advertisers perfected the strategies of using children to influence mothers' purchasing. Meanwhile, other factors contributed to defining children as a specialized consumer market including the growing professions of child psychology and market research, the rapidly expanding population of children, and, of course, the general place of advertising in a profit-driven media environment. Advertisers and product manufacturers saw the medium of radio as an important venue for promoting products to children. The financial support for radio programs moved quickly from sustaining (support by the station or network) to sponsored (support by advertisers) with product and personality tie-ins and promotions used to encourage attention (West, 1988). It is important to note that the products advertised on children's radio programs were often household goods from national corporations. Advertisers on early children's radio included food companies such as the Kellogg Company, General Mills, Campbell Soup, and the Quaker Oats Company; cleaning products such as Spic and Span and Bon Ami; and oil companies such as the Pure Oil Company, Standard Oil, and Sinclair Oil (Grumbine, 1938). They all offered premiums and contests with rewards of toys, but, as a rule, toy companies did not advertise on radio.

In addition to being influences on family purchasing, children were seen as future consumers. The prevailing notion was it was the parents' duty to teach children the value of money; such teachings were seen as essential to the development of healthy individuals (Gruenberg & Gruenberg, 1933; Grumbine, 1935a, 1935b, 1938). High schools conducted consumer education programs advocating fiscal responsibility (McNeal, 1987), and the popular press featured stories of the importance of financial responsibility (Blatz, 1933; Gruenberg, 1934; Gruenberg & Gruenberg, 1931; O'Donnell, 1930). The White House Conference on Child Health and Protection, held in 1930, reported a relationship between delinquency and allowance, with nondelinquent boys more likely to receive an allowance than predelinquent boys (Zelizer, 1985). This was, no doubt, a rather simplistic analysis of the factors contributing to delinquency, but it points out the value attributed to some form of income for young children.

Other experts also promoted the importance of socializing children as consumers:

> The child's right to choose his own clothes and the furniture for his own room is not a passing fad. It is founded solidly in the newer knowledge of child psychology. . . . Wearing the wrong thing because mother thinks it is "so cute" can develop a real inferiority complex that may take years to outgrow. (Grumbine, 1938, p. 359)

These were the beginnings of what would become increasingly sophisticated explanations of the child-consumer, based on expert opinion from professionals in the field of child development, psychology, and market research. People such as Sidonie Gruenberg and E. Evalyn Grumbine were a part of the new discipline of child psychology, interested in the pragmatic application of these theories to the training of children. Gruenberg was director of the Child Study Association and lecturer in Parent Education at Columbia University, Teachers College; Grumbine was the author of one of the few comprehensive tracts for advertisers in the 1930s, *Reaching Juvenile Markets,* thus positioning each as authorities. According to Grumbine (1935a), "An understanding of children, of their physical and mental development, their likes and dislikes and their reactions to the rapidly changing conditions of living today, will help manufacturers to plan better advertising campaigns" (p. 28).

This "understanding" she spoke of came from the growing field of child development and child psychology. As early as 1931, people such as the Gruenbergs and Grumbine were working toward the practical application of these theories to consumer behavior.

During this time, children were considered active consumers of small items, such as candy, toys, and foods (especially cereals), but they were not considered important influences on major family purchases (Gruenberg & Gruenberg, 1933; Grumbine, 1938). Children's purchasing power, reflected in the products advertised to them on radio, was seen as limited to disposable goods relevant to their immediate needs and consumption.

Table 1.1 is a listing of nationally advertised products during the first decade of radio broadcasting on programs classified as child-oriented shows.[2]

Only Anacin and Pepsodent toothpaste were not food products; consequently, 30 of the 32 fully sponsored, nationally distributed children's programs during the first decade of radio were supported by food companies, and all programs were sponsored by household products, considering aspirin (Anacin) and toothpaste (Pepsodent) as household goods.

During the 1920s and 1930s, some of the major trends in children's consumerization were established: (1) the use of media markets to reach parents through children; (2) the application of "experts" and research to understanding consumer behavior; and (3) the targeting of food products and household goods to children, either to influence parents' purchases or to expand potential markets.

TABLE 1.1. Nationally Advertised Products on Network Radio, 1930–1939

	Product	Program
1930–1934	Book House	*Story Time*
	Dromedary	*Desert Caravan*
	Davis Baking	*Flying Family*
	General Foods	*Paul Wing the Story Man*
	General Mills	*Skippy*
		Jack Armstrong
	Jello	*Wizard of Oz*
	Kellogg	*Singing Lady*
	Kreml	*Uncle Ollie and His Gang*
	Maltex	*Safety Soldiers*
	Maltine	*Maltine Story Time*
	Ovaltine	*Little Orphan Annie*
	Phillips	*Skippy*
	Ralston	*Sekatary Hawkins*
		Tom Mix
	Wrigley Gum	*Lone Wolf Tribe*
1935–1939	Anacin	*Junior Nurse Corps*
	Bond Bread	*Terry and Ted*
	Dari Rich	*Terry and the Pirates*
	General Mills	*Jack Armstrong*
	Kellogg	*Singing Lady*
		Don Winslow of the Navy
		Tom Mix
	Ovaltine	*Little Orphan Annie*
	Pepsodent	*Mickey Mouse Theater*
	Puffed Wheat	*Dick Tracy*
	Quaker Oats	*Dick Tracy*
	Ralston	*Tom Mix*
	Tastee Bread	*Omar, the Mystic*
	Wheatena	*Popeye, the Sailor*
		Jack Armstrong
		Dorothy Gordon, Stories
	Wheaties	*Jack Armstrong*

Note. Sponsored children's programs, daytime comedies and thrillers (Monday through Friday, 3:00–6:00 P.M., or Saturday morning). Data compiled from Summers (1971).

1940 to 1950

The 1940s found the country preoccupied with World War II, and advertising tended to focus on conservation and nationalism (McNeal, 1987). However, it was also the beginning of more aggressive marketing to young people. Previously, agencies had not specialized in children's advertising or market research.

This growing interest in the youth market was influenced by new technology (television) and social change (the baby boom). The young population had steadily increased both in numbers and percentages since the 1920s, with the most dramatic changes during the late 1940s and 1950s, with each child representing a potential consumer.

Specialty magazines such as *Seventeen*, first published in 1944, and radio were the primary advertising media during this time (Shaffer, 1965).

Sponsorship of radio in the 1940s and early 1950s looked much like radio of the 1930s, and, as illustrated in Table 1.2, many of the same goods advertised to children of the 1930s were advertised to children of the 1940s.

Again, all but a very few sponsors—Buster Brown Shoes, Shaeffer Pens, and Lever Brothers—represented food products. Of the 41 nationally sponsored programs, 36 were sponsored by foods. By 1955, there were no nationally distributed radio programs scheduled for children; the audience had turned to television.

As television became a reality in the 1950s and market researchers were recognizing the value of children as consumers, professionals such as Dr. Spock were encouraging parents to allow children more freedom and responsibility. At one level, that translated to decisions in family purchases. In addition to candy and toys, advertisers were encouraged to market household furnishings, televisions, cameras, and automobiles to the growing youth population (Gilbert, 1957; "Youth," 1964), and parents were encouraged to include children in the discussion about these purchases. At that time, Gilbert, a leader in children's marketing research, outlined three approaches to marketing that he defined as "forward looking," and, indeed, they are still important to children's marketing practices.

(1) Expand the youth market on seasonal items—toys, ice cream, wearing apparel.[3]

TABLE 1.2. Nationally Advertised Products on Network Radio, 1940–1955

	Product	Program
1940–1944	Buster Brown Shoes	*Smiling Ed McConnell*
	Cream of Wheat	*Let's Pretend*
	General Foods	*Hop Harrigan*
	General Mills	*Jack Armstrong*
	Kellogg	*Superman*
	Ovaltine	*Captain Midnight*
	Quaker Oats	*Terry and the Pirates*
	Ralston	*Tom Mix*
	Sweets Co.	*Dick Tracy*
	Wheaties	*Jack Armstrong*
1945–1949	Bosco	*Land of the Lost*
	Buster Brown Shoes	*Smiling Ed McConnell*
	Cream of Wheat	*Let's Pretend*
	Derby Foods	*Sky King*
	General Foods	*Hop Harrigan*
		Buck Rogers
	General Mills	*Jack Armstrong*
	Kellogg	*Superman*
	Lever Brothers	*Junior Miss*
	M&M Candies	*Joe DiMaggio: Sports Dramas*
	Nabisco	*Straight Arrow*
	Ovaltine	*Captain Midnight*
	Quaker Oats	*Terry and the Pirates*
		Challenge of the Yukon
	Ralston	*Tom Mix*
	Shaeffer Pens	*Adventure Club*
	Swift Packaging	*Archie Andrews*
		Meet the Meeks
	Ward Baking	*Tennessee Jed*
1950–1954	Buster Brown Shoes	*Smiling Ed McConnell*
	Cream of Wheat	*Let's Pretend*
	Derby Foods	*Sky King*
	Grass Noodles	*Super Noodle*
	Kellogg	*Clyde Beatty Adventures*
		Mark Trail
		Tom Corbett: Space Cadet
		Wild Bill Hickok
	Kraft Foods	*Bobby Benson*
	Nabisco	*Straight Arrow*
	Nestlé	*Space Patrol*
	Orange Crush	*Green Hornet*
	Quaker Oats	*Sergeant Preston of the Yukon*
	Ralston	*Space Patrol*

Note. Sponsored children's programs, daytime comedies and thrillers (Monday through Friday, 3:00–6:00 P.M., or Saturday morning). Data compiled from Summers (1971).

(2) Develop special projects for youth—something to be used in adult form; watches, typewriters, face creams; to develop brand loyalty.

(3) Adapt marketing approaches—products not particularly designed for the youth market but they will purchase in the future: automobiles, television sets, foods. (Gilbert, 1957, p. 52)

Soon, these suggestions were a part of the new trend in youth-oriented marketing. Adult products were advertised to teens: A soap company spoke to young girls, saying, "You'll be using make-up soon, that's why you should use Dial" (Gilbert, 1957). Brand loyalty was promoted as clothing merchants introduced name brands, and automobile companies built name recognition by providing material for high-school courses (Shaffer, 1965).

Stories such as the success of Welch's Grape Juice, sold during the 1930s as a diet drink and marketed as a family product in the 1950s, were used to change marketing strategies.

> Since emphasis on family means in most cases families with children, Welch signed up with the *Howdy Doody Show*, with which it was connected until 1954; then it moved over to Walt Disney's *Mickey Mouse Club* until 1956. During its sponsorship of the *Howdy Doody Show*, the consumption of grape juice rose sharply in families with children aged 5 to 11 . . . from some 8 million dollars in 1949 to almost 37 million for the 1955–1956 fiscal year. (Gilbert, 1957, p. 120)

Advertisers were working to expand and increase the market, develop brand loyalty, and establish a future interest. As an influential market, many seemingly irrelevant products were advertised to children and teenagers.

1960 to 1970

The 1960s were an important time for children's marketing: Both the birthrate and family incomes were increasing, and the first agency to specialize in children's advertising, Helitzer,

Waring and Wayne, opened in 1963 (Helitzer, personal communication, September 1996). The baby boom of the late 1940s and early 1950s created a numerically larger market. The growing economy gave families more discretionary income, and increasingly, advertisers looked to persuade children to consider their products (Shaffer, 1965).

Among the most important of these factors was the growing teen population that was a result of the baby boom.

> The adolescent's pervasive effect on the consumer market is derived in large part from the characteristic traits of the individual at this time of life—a big appetite, restless energy, passion for vehicles, receptivity to fads, worry about personal appearance, etc. . . .
>
> Teen-agers are reported to drink 3½ billion quarts of milk a year . . . to make half a billion telephone calls a week . . . 81 per cent of teen-agers owned radios, 78 per cent owned watches, 49 per cent had record players. . . . Teen-agers and those a bit older were responsible for 55 per cent of all soft drink sales, 53 per cent of movie ticket sales, 44 per cent of camera sales, 43 per cent of record sales, and 26 per cent of cosmetic sales. (Shaffer, 1965, p. 630)

Two events occurred during the 1970s that legitimized this new consumer market—both the government and academia took notice. As an extension of the consumer rights movement of the 1960s, the Federal Trade Commission became particularly vigilant with regard to children's advertising (McNeal, 1987). In addition children's consumer behavior gained the attention of those doing academic research in institutions as prestigious as the Harvard University School of Business (McNeal, 1987).

An analysis of the research on children and the media from 1900 to 1990 found over 1,400 citations on the topic.[4] Children's advertising was the subject of 143 studies, considering a range of issues including media content, social effects, and consumer behavior. As demonstrated in Table 1.3, although there were over 300 studies on children and the media, prior to 1970, virtually no academic research was conducted on children's advertising (see also McNeal, 1987). After 1970, advertising research becomes a more notable percent of children's media research.

Advertising research of the 1970s and 1980s was a part of the general growth of research on children. A few researchers, including McNeal, began to address the topic in the 1950s and 1960s; in the 1970s, with the increasing attention to the role of media in children's lives, attention was also drawn to the child consumer. Sanctioned by government hearings and investigations before the Federal Trade Commission, colleges were inclined to support research on the question.

One of the consequences of this attention was a more sophisticated understanding of the child. In the tradition of the Gruenbergs, and Grumbine, and others of the 1930s, psychologists, sociologists, economists, and communications scholars added new theoretical frames to guide market research. Based on an analysis of academic research conducted by McNeal in 1987, there was a wide range of work examining children as consumers from these scholars (McNeal, 1987, Table 8.1, p. 140).

As the work of the early academics demonstrated, through the practical application of theoretical principles, such work finds its way to market research. Consequently, the 1970s presented a more complex understanding of the child consumer.

TABLE 1.3. Media-Related Research on Children and Advertising, 1900–1989

	Total studies	Advertising studies only	Percent advertising
1930–1939	102	3	2.9
1940–1949	66	0	0
1950–1959	104	5	4.8
1960–1969	131	6	4.6
1970–1979	498	64	12.9
1980–1989	530	65	12.3
Total	1,431	143	

Note. Data compiled by Wartella and Pecora.

1980 to 1990

By the 1980s, children were still perceived as the *primary* consumers for a variety of products: candy (58%) and toys (30%); and *influential* in the purchase decisions of clothing (about 80%), sneakers (72%), toys (80%), cereal (65%), video movies (45%), and toothpaste (30%) (Stipp, 1988). However, as the market and the conceptualization of children changed over time, there was a growing consideration of the child as a sophisticated consumer—"well informed and media-wise" (Weisskoff, 1985, p. RC-13).

One advertising executive, talking about teenagers, identified the differences between children of the 1930s and children of the 1980s: "They are very disciplined about acquiring money, very goal oriented. But there is a major change in the work ethic. It's no longer work hard and save for a brighter future. Now it is work hard and get what you want today" (Trachtenberg, 1986, p. 201)

Character licensing and the growth of specialty stores such as Toys 'R' Us expanded the range of products available and appealed to this fancy to spend. Now the toy, fast-food, and clothing industries competed with companies such as General Mills and General Foods for the young market. In 1975, Barcus found that 17.3% of the Saturday morning advertisements were for toys; in a 1991 replication, toy ads accounted for 29.5% of the Saturday morning commercials (Pecora, 1991).

The 1990s brought a further segmentation of the market, with a renewed interest in teens and a new-market of "tweens." Tweens (10- to 13-year-olds) were identified as those not given the independence allowed teenagers but already interested in the consumer goods and services available to their older brothers and sisters. They often spend Saturday afternoon at the mall but have to be home by dinner. Among the first products clearly marketed to this group were clothing and snack foods, but, increasingly, corporations such as IBM and Sony have begun to recognize their purchasing potential, both current and future: Toothpaste, easy-to-prepare meals, electronic equipment, and deodorants are just a few of the goods sold to this group.

Projected to increase in the late 1990s (Stipp, 1993) as the service industries supplied larger numbers of low-paying jobs, the expendable income of teenagers will continue to increase (Miller, 1990; Schwartz, 1990). It has been predicted that in the future, segmentation of the children's market will not only be based on age but also on household income, media habits, geography, and lifestyle (McNeal, 1992a, 1992b).

As we move into the 21st century, children are well-trained consumers able to associate Ronald McDonald with good things before they have learned the language. Market segmentation is consistent with a shift in general consumer patterns from family needs and wants to individual consumption (Hollander & Germain, 1992). Initially, children were brought into the consumer movement to influence family purchasing behavior. By the late 1930s, advertisers recognized that children were consumers in their own right, with purchasing decisions generally limited to items such as candy and cereal. When television was established in the mid-1950s, children continued to be an important market for these goods while experts argued children should be given the freedom to make their own decisions and choices—a boon to advertisers. Children were now seen as more self-sufficient in purchasing decisions. Not only was their increased income and influence on family purchasing recognized as important to consumerism, but also the idea was that if they could be attracted to a product at a young age, they would remain loyal customers when they became older and "real" consumers. They were sophisticated consumers, although not particularly brand-loyal (Helitzer & Heyel, 1970). By the 1980s, children were selecting their own brands—well before they could read, they could identify Ronald McDonald and all he represents ("Now Billy," 1983; Guber, 1985). This fostered a loyalty to icons encouraged by the introduction of tie-ins: product merchandising and media characters. Sneakers were no longer bought because of cost or quality, but it was the novelty of a readily identifiable symbol such as the Little Mermaid that made them salable.

CONNECTIONS: PRODUCTS AND PROGRAMS

Over the years, as children were learning to be consumers, they became important as audiences to an advertising-driven medium such as radio and later to television. The union of a consumer market—children—and a commercial medium—radio—to form an audience for advertisers was a "natural." One of the ways of attracting children was the use of age-specific adventure stories and entertainment; another was through the use of premiums and tie-ins. A tie-in, the promotion of a product and a media event by linking the two, is not a new phenomenon. Early in its history, the motion picture industry recognized its influence on the material nature of the young: It is rumored that Shirley Temple earned more in the sales of clothing and dolls than she did from her motion pictures (Seldes, 1938). As radio became a major children's entertainment source, such tie-ins served to the advantage of both product and program. Table 1.4, complied from market reports at the NBC radio network, identifies a few of the earliest program and product tie-ins.

Dick Tracy decoder rings and Little Orphan Annie mugs were some of the most treasured premiums offered. However, radio sponsors also offered Buck Rogers club memberships, maps, and cutouts; CoCoMalt weight-gain charts; Bobby Benson club memberships, lasso and lariats; and Inspector Post Junior Detective Corps detective manual.

Perhaps the most successful of these media tie-in campaigns was organized by the Hecker H-O Cereal Company. In

TABLE 1.4. Advertised Products and Radio Programs, 1932

Program	Sponsor	Premium/tie in
Happy Wonder Bakers	Wonder Bread	Happy Wonder Sandwich Book
Jolly Bill and Jane	Cream of Wheat	HCB[a] club membership
Quaker Early Birds	Quaker Oats Company	Rag doll
Little Orphan Annie	Ovaltine	Annie's picture

Note. Data compiled from NBC Statistical Department (1932) and NBC Merchandising Division (1933).
[a]Hot Cereal Breakfast.

1932, it sponsored a radio show about the life of Bobby Benson, an 11-year-old boy who inherited a ranch.

> Before the initial broadcast of the H-Bar-O Rangers in September, 1932, more than 1,200 husky cowboys appeared regularly in the vicinity of schools and playgrounds. Throughout the residential sections of cities within the distribution territory of the company was heard—"The H-Bar-O Rangers are coming." . . . Cowboy shows were staged during the week before the first broadcast. . . . This merchandising in advance made boys and girls look forward to the program. (Grumbine, 1935a, pp. 31–32)

Today, promoting products or programs or the character-of-the-day, live models of characters such as Strawberry Shortcake, Papa Smurf, the Teenage Mutant Ninja Turtles, or the Power Rangers can be found wherever there are large groups of children. In the 1980s, a group of singing chipmunks were the center of a campaign similar to Bobby Benson's 50 years earlier. *The Chipmunk Adventure* was a feature-film released with tie-ins that included Burger King glasses, Disney records, and General Mills cereal products. As with Bobby Benson's singing cowboys, the Chipmunks toured the country, covering more than 25 major markets but, where the singing cowboys appeared at playgrounds, the Chipmunks made their debut at that modern-day playground, the shopping mall ("Promo Tie-Ins," 1987).

Another way in which program and product links are encouraged builds on the importance of "collecting" in children's play. Identified as early as the 1930s, the child as pack rat has been the foundation of many products available today. "The collecting instinct is almost universal. From about three years of age the child begins to acquire small objects of various kinds. The greatest activity is between eight and fifteen years, with the ten-year-old probably the most intensive collector" (Grumbine, 1935b, p. 36).

These days, these collectibles are characters such as My Little Pony, the Smurfs, Strawberry Shortcake, and G. I. Joe and their many friends. Grumbine discussed the collecting instinct in terms of stamps, leaves, cutouts, and marbles; however, toy manufacturers appeal to this stage with a myriad of media heroes—each sold separately. This phenomenon has been an important marketing concept encouraged by animated programming. Each program plot can identify a new character to be added to a child's collection at the next birthday or the next trip to the store.

Tie-ins and promotions serve a very important function for both the market and the media. For the market, they bring product awareness. A child sees the toy–cereal–candy–clothing on the shelf and can make connections with attractive, exciting recognizable characters from the media. Images of the Little Mermaid on a pair of shoes transforms a pair of ordinary sneakers to LITTLE MERMAID SNEAKERS, a possession to be envied and discussed over milk and cookies at day care. Conversely, the pair of Little Mermaid sneakers leads to a recognition of the Little Mermaid video, television program, motion picture, or storybook. One pair of sneakers encourages consumer and audience.

2

♦♦♦

Children Become Audiences

Children of the radio era were considered "natural and enthusiastic buyers," a responsive audience with "tremendous sales potential" for advertisers (Grumbine, 1938). But it was television and its "intimate and persuasive selling power . . . [that] appeared more effective than perhaps any other advertising force in its impact upon youngsters" (Niefeld, cited in Gilbert, 1957, p. 124)

However, it was not the first. Beginning with the introduction of mass-produced magazines and dime novels in the 1890s, children have been a part of the media audience. Pamphlets, trading cards and paper cutouts, distributed as advertisements, were popular in the 1900s (Strasser, 1989). Among the more interesting of these was a widely distributed storybook published by Bon Ami, a household cleaning product. The story of *The Chick That Never Grew Up* featured the Princess Bon Ami and was dedicated to "the millions of children whose mothers find Bon Ami a good friend" (Davey, 1926)

By the introduction of motion pictures, children were an important constituency of the media. Later, when radio became an entertainment medium, children were already established as a potential audience.

Although there has been, from the beginning, a concern with the influence of these media on social development, our interest here is with the way children are viewed as a media audience in the marketplace.

To understand the child audience, it is important to understand the children's media marketplace. If one accepts the fact that the value or importance of an audience can be predicted by the attention paid to them by those in the media industries, then the growth of children's radio programming, as a part of the general growth of radio, serves as one of the first indications of children's importance as an audience. In 1928, there were only three daily programs for children on the four New York metropolitan-area radio stations; within 5 years, 52 programs were aired daily on the four stations (Grumbine, 1938). On network radio, the number of hours of children's radio programming increased from 300 programs in 1930 to over 1,000 in 1933 (Grumbine, 1938). Many of these programs began without advertising, supported by the station, "to interest and entertain boys and girls, and at the same time to satisfy parents" (Grumbine, 1938, p. 222). As audience numbers and programming availability grew, product manufacturers took over program sponsorship (Summers, 1971).

Television maintained the tradition of radio in terms of both form and structure. Early children's television programs were based on radio serials like *Flash Gordon* and were offered during the same time schedule.

By the 1970s, the skyrocketing cost of program production and distribution, and increased competition for advertising dollars changed the makeup of the entertainment media industries. Among these changes was the inclusion of new investors with whom to share the economic risk in an increasingly expensive game. This led to the growth of large media corporations or conglomerates that claim ownership in several facets of the business and coproduction arrangements that will be considered later. For the children's entertainment market, fragmentation was initiated with the growth of independent stations and the introduction of alternative markets such as cable and videocassette. Fragmentation is addressed here as an increase in media outlets. While the media market was undergoing the changes that led to conglomerization and fragmentation, the toy industry also underwent significant shifts, the most important here was the move from an industry driven by fluctuating sales, mostly in the fourth quarter (Christmas) to a year-round, consumer-driven market encouraged by the growing industry of character licensing.[1] Where once there were three national networks, there were now multiple media outlets; where once each industry, media and toy, was relatively autonomous, they were now collaborative. Internationalization was the consequence of further market expansion and will be discussed in a later chapter.

Changes in market structure led industries to diversify corporate holdings, spread the risk of economic failure, and capitalize on financial gain through mutually beneficial arrangements. In the toy and media industries, these arrangements take the shape of cooperation in product development, character or merchandise licensing agreements, or outright ownership of program syndication by the toy company ("Mattel Toys Debuts," 1986). It has been agreements such as these that led to the increase of children's merchandise based on characters designed for their possibilities as toys and cartoons.

These economic arrangements become problematic in a regulated industry like broadcasting, where the vagaries of the marketplace are subject to the regulatory influence of the government. Therefore, to understand the business of children's entertainment, it is important to recognize the significance of the regulatory process that is often used in attempts to manage what children read, hear, or see.

THE ROLE OF GOVERNMENT

The role of government (Federal Communications Commission, Federal Trade Commission, and Congress) must be considered in any discussion of children's media. For example, the special status of the child has often been used as a rallying cry to improve media for the child audience. Yet little change has been brought about by governmental regulation notwithstanding the legion of hearings held on children's entertainment including comic books, television, records, and video games. In most instances, change has been the result of self-regulation brought on by the *threat* of government intervention. The comic book, recording, and video-game industries all have imposed some form of industrywide standards after government attention. The one exception is the Children's Television Act of 1990, yet, even here, it has taken over 5 years to set the industrywide standards called for in the Act.

Among the earliest attempts at governmental intervention was the Post Office's attack on dime novels. In the 1870s, concerned with the material available to young boys, Anthony Comstock was instrumental in passing a congressional act entitled "An Act for the Suppression of Trade in, and Circulation of, Obscene Literature and Articles of Immoral Use." Over his lifetime, he used this legislation, and his position as Director and special agent in the Post Office, to regulate material sent through the mails, including the dime novels so popular with young boys (Bremmer, 1967). Other early regulation was generally addressed at the local level, when cities or states sought to impose censorship laws or health regulations to supervise children's use of the motion pictures (Short, 1928). Children's interests in broadcasting were not formally addressed by the Federal Government until the 1950s, when the Congressional Hearings on juvenile delinquency investigated the role of comic books, motion pictures, and television. Beginning with Comstock and through to the 1950s, the primary concern was with the contribution of media content to children's potential for violence (Reeves & Baughman, 1983; Rowland, 1983), a concern that continues. Consequently, the primary interest has been interest with media content or behavioral effects, not the economics of the children's media industry.

It was not until the 1960s that attention turned to the economics of children's broadcasting, when they were defined as a part of the standards for license renewal (Cole & Oettinger, 1978; Neff, 1994). Also during the 1970s and 1980s, numerous hearings on children's advertising and programming were held by the Federal Trade Commission, the Federal Communications Commission, and in the Senate and the House of Representatives (MacGregor, 1984; Thorburn, 1990; Kunkel & Roberts, 1991). The intent of the majority of these hearings was to regulate the children's media marketplace by setting standards on advertising or advertising minutes or amount of program availability.

However, change is not always brought about in obvious ways. Notwithstanding the numerous governmental hearings on children's media, it was regulation that sought to break up the three networks' domination of the industry that brought about the most significant change. During the 1970s, the Prime-Time Access Rule and the Financial and Syndication Interest Rulings were instituted to give greater access to independent production companies (Brown, 1986). These ruling came out of the antitrust environment of the 1950s and a concern with the increasing control of program production and the syndication market by the three networks (Litman, 1979).

The intent of the rulings was to limit the power of the three networks. The Prime-Time Access Rule was to open up the market to local stations by limiting network control of prime time, the Financial Interest Rule was to limit the financial benefits accrued by network program production investments, and the Syndication Rule was to limit the networks' investment in program syndication. These regulations resulted in a growth of syndicated programming and financing through barter agreements and, incidentally, an increase in the number of independent television stations across the country.[2] Low up-front costs through barter arrangements made first-run syndicated programming available to the independent television stations, allowing them to compete with the networks for audience and advertising dollars.[3] Because independent stations programmed heavily for children, among the first programming to benefit from these changes was children's cartoons. In 1977, the primary syndicated children's programming available was old theatrical cartoons, formerly shown in movie houses, or off-network cartoons that had a previous life on a Saturday morning network schedule ("Children's TV," 1977); by 1985, in addition to the previous programs, several cartoon programs made specifically for the first-run market on independent stations were available. Several of these programs, such as *She-Ra: Princess of Power, Terrahawks, ThunderCats,* and *Transformers* were shows associated with toy products.

In part this was the consequence of a 1983 Federal Communications Commission Report and Order (55RR2d) that rescinded its 1974 policy statement on children's programming, thus legitimizing product-based programs. The debate centered around the value of programs based on licensed characters and the definition of such programs as "entertainment" or "commercial." Representatives of the entertainment and toy industry claimed that such programs offered positive social messages; public interest groups argued that they were simply 30 minutes of product advertisement. The debate over children's television became mired in "minutes of commercials" rather than the implications of a commercial children's entertainment venue.

HISTORY OF CHILDREN'S PROGRAMMING[4]

When television became a part of the entertainment industries in the late 1940s, it was built on the model of network radio, a national, commercial broadcasting system that offered an easy transition to the new technology of television. According to Turow (1981):

> The business activities of the major television networks in the late 1940s and early 1950s were guided, to an important degree, by the firms' experiences in radio. They realized that television had the same potential as radio for becoming an important advertising medium. (p. 18)

Figure 2.1 demonstrates the variation in the *number* of television programs offered for children over the years. It is argued

Number of programs

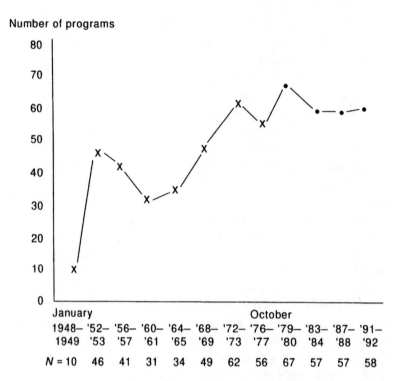

FIGURE 2.1. Children's television programs on national networks: ABC, CBS, NBC. *Sources:* (×) Turow (1981, pp. 23, 56, 91); (•) Pecora (unpublished data, 1994). Turow data based on *The New York Times* January television listings; author data based on *TV Guide* for October. Turow's unit of analysis was based on a 2-year span to compensate for yearly vagaries (p. 23). The later years continue that model.

that these shifts serve as an indicator of the value of the child audience—higher numbers indicate more value. There are several points at which the networks increased the number of programs offered to children. Between 1950 and 1952, 1970 and 1972, and in the late 1970s, there are interesting increases in the number of programs offered. The first increase can be explained by the industry's attempt to reach the adult purchasing audience through children. The early 1970s growth in programming can be accounted for as a response to more sophisticated ratings numbers and the threat of regulation from an active Federal Communications Commission. The late 1970s increase was probably a response to a general increase in programming.

Until the mid-1950s, the child audience was instrumental in promoting television ownership in the home. Once the number of homes with television reached a majority, the child audience was replaced with programming to adult consumers, who were more valuable to advertisers. Consequently, there was a drop in programming for children during the late 1950s and the 1960s. Figure 2.1 represents all programs aired during one week. What it does not reflect is the move of children's programming from weekday evenings to Saturday mornings and the subtle shifts, such as NBC's move to an older audience in the early 1990s. In the mid-1960s, as the child audience gained in numbers and expendable income, they again had value as an audience and more programming became available. By the 1990s, there were cable networks, where a large percentage of the programming was aimed at the child audience.

The Early Years

Like early radio, children's television was first sponsored on a sustaining basis; programs were defined by the networks as promotional material. Of the programs offered during the first 4 years of television, over half received some support from the networks (Melody, 1973; Turow, 1980). The child audience was used to encourage the sales of television, selling parents on the educational and prosocial possibilities of the new technology. Once most households had a television set, there was no longer a need to attract a young viewing audience, sustaining program production was no longer practical, and stations went after the audience with income—adults. However, for some time slots, there was very little adult audience; grown-ups were assumed to be doing other things. So, the use of Saturday mornings to program for children was precipitated by the need to use equipment and time, and to attract some audience, any audience, that might bring in advertising income. It was not cost-effective to program for this nonexistent audience (adults), but children were perceived to be available, and, consequently, time could be sold to advertisers with goods to promote to children (Melody, 1973). During the first years of television, 80% of all children's programming was scheduled for the early evening hours, but, gradually, the market moved to Saturday morning.

By the mid-1950s, television's penetration in the home reached near saturation levels, and there was no longer the need to promote sales (Adler, 1980). The television audience shifted from potential buyers of television sets to potential consumers of advertised goods; children were now perceived as only incidental to the consumer market.

1960 to 1970

During the 1960s, children's programming again underwent change as the market potential of children gained in recognition. Advertisers began to rely more heavily on ratings data; prime-time programming was established as the premier family format, and cartoons became an important source of low-cost children's entertainment. Improvements in the collection of ratings data gave a more sophisticated picture of the audience, the data supplied advertisers with an understanding of audience segmentation, allowing them to make more exact decisions about commercial placement (Beville, 1985).

The broadcast networks recognized the marketability of the child audience to the advertisers, though they were still not as valuable an audience as their parents (Shelby, 1964; Turow, 1980). During 1960–1961, there were 10 prime-time children's programs scheduled, but by 1965, the number of prime-time children's programs dropped as the networks shifted the child audience to Saturday morning. Since then, there has been no regularly scheduled, prime-time children's entertainment, though there have been occasional specials and children, of course, watch dramas such as *MacGuyver* and situation comedies such as *Full House*.

In addition, the factors that promoted a young consumer market also encouraged a young audience. As Melody explained the phenomenon: As advertisers discovered the $50 billion market and the accent on youth encouraged the demand for Saturday morning programming, Nielsen ratings demonstrated that on Saturday morning "advertisers could reach a thousand children ... for $1.00, whereas weekdays they would only reach 286 children for their dollar, and in prime time only 133 kids" (1973, p. 51).[5] Furthermore, according to Melody (1973):

> Children's television had emerged as a full contender in the ratings and revenue competition between the networks. As this market became more and more lucrative, the profit opportunities for competitive market shares increased. The payoff for gaining or losing in the ratings was becoming increasingly great. Hence, the children's schedule was attracting more and more careful attention as a device for profitability delivering child audiences to specific advertisers. (pp. 51–52)

Perhaps the major debate over children's television during the 1970s was its commercialization. Reacting to the limited programming and increasing commercialization of children's programming, Action for Children's Television sought to establish standards in the industry. The group petitioned the Federal Communications Commission, requesting three changes: (1) age-specific children's programming, (2) limits on the number of minutes of advertising, and (3) the elimination of host selling. Host selling was eliminated but, although the issue of age-specific programming continues to be addressed, public discussions about children's television during this decade most often focused on commercial minutes per hour.

While this particular debate continues, other forces came together that had consequences for the child audience. The size of the television audience grew from 87% of all households owning a television in 1960 to 95% owning sets in 1970, representing a new audience of over 14 million households (Sterling & Kittross, 1990).

The three networks expanded the Saturday morning hours extending the available commercial time (Turow, 1981). Between 1967 and 1977, ABC and NBC added 90 minutes to their Saturday schedule and CBS added 2 hours (Grossman,

1980). Overall programming hours increased from 22.08 hours of children's series on the three networks in the 1966–1967 season to 36.08 hours in the 1976–1977 season (Turow, 1981).

It was also during the 1970s that the impact of the Prime-Time Access Rule and Financial and Syndication Rulings on children's programming became evident. The number of independent stations increased, creating a demand for programming and making more commercial minutes available (Frazier Gross and Kadlec Inc., 1986).

1980 to 1990

The 1980s brought several changes to children's television; in addition to new markets, there were changes in programming and sponsorship forms. It is at this point that the line between sponsorship and program became blurred as producers, looking to spread the risk of program production costs, turned to toy manufacturers, and toy manufacturers, wanting to stabilize a market subject to children's whim and fancy, turned to the media. Shows were developed with the consultation, and in some instances, financial backing, of toy manufacturers and licensing agents.

The independent television stations became an outlet for this genre of programming, generally animated, that was tied to preexisting or new toys.[6] These programs not only attracted an audience but also encouraged brand awareness: The *Strawberry Shortcake* television special served as an advertisement for Strawberry Shortcake T-shirts, activity books, storybooks, the videocassette, and sneakers. In a market of intense competition, these product-based programs minimized risk both in production costs and ratings. The cost of producing the program could be spread between program producers and product manufacturer or licenser, and recognition of either the product merchandise or the program increases sales and ratings.

Table 2.1 illustrates the expansion of these properties between 1980 and 1985; the first year of a truly "toy-based" program was 1983 with the Filmation/Mattel property *He-Man and the Masters of the Universe*.

TABLE 2.1. Animated Programming by Source on Independent Stations in the New York Metropolitan Area, 1982–1985

Off-network programs	Theatrical cartoons	Product-based programs
	1982	
Bullwinkle	*Cartoon Festival*	
Flintstones	*Popeye*	
Josie and the Pussycats	*Sylvester and Tweety*	
Magilla Gorilla	*Tom and Jerry*	
Pink Panther		
Return to the Planet of the Apes		
Scooby Doo		
	1983	
Blackstar	*Bugs and Porky*	*He-Man*
Bullwinkle	*Popeye*	*Strawberry Shortcake*
Flintstones	*Tom and Jerry*	
Josie and the Pussycats	*Woody Woodpecker*	
Pink Panther		
Return to the Planet of the Apes		
Scooby Doo		
Superfriends		
	1984	
Battle of the Planets	*Bugs and Porky*	*The Gobots*
Bullwinkle	*Popeye*	*He-Man*
Flintstones	*Tom and Jerry*	*Poochie*
Pink Panther	*Woody Woodpecker*	*Transformers*
Plastic Man		*Voltron*
Return to the Planet of the Apes		
Scooby Doo		
Superfriends		
	1985	
Battle of the Planets	*Popeye*	*G.I. Joe*
Flintstones	*Tom and Jerry*	*The Gobots*
Jetsons	*Woody Woodpecker*	*He-Man*
Josie and the Pussycats		*Mask*
Plastic Man		*She-Ra*
Return to the Planet of the Apes		*Terrahawks*
Scooby Doo		*ThunderCats*
Superfriends		*Transformers*
		Voltron

Note: Data compiled from *TV Guide* (October 18–22, 1982; October 22–28, 1983; October 27–November 2, 1984; October 12–18, 1985).

By the 1990s, the children's television environment included cable and premium stations not available earlier. The 1970 market was limited to the three national networks with independent stations in some of the major metropolitan markets. By the mid-1980s independent stations and specialized networks such as the Disney Channel and Nickelodeon were available to those with access to cable television.[7] Turow (1981) found there were 36.9 hours of network children's programs in 1970 and, with an additional 48 hours in local children's programming in New York City, the largest television market, children could watch 85 more hours in that one week. Twenty years later, in 1990, those children would have had almost 300 hours of television available in one week.[8]

In an effort to further expand the market during the 1990s, stations began programming to attract a "tween" audience. Programmers targeted this audience of children between ages 9 and 12 by filling the late afternoon time-period with off-network sitcoms, reality-based programs, game shows, and teen soaps such as *Swan's Crossing* or serials based on familiar books characters such as Nancy Drew and the girls of the *Baby-Sitters Club*. For fall 1990, NBC replaced its traditional Saturday morning cartoon lineup with live-action programs that typically attract an older youth audience. According to one NBC senior vice-president, this was a conscious strategy to pursue teens and tweens through live action (Blickstein, 1992).

The children's entertainment market now included a proliferation of programs and outlets not considered when television first came into the home. The media marketplace was comprised of independent television stations, cable networks, syndicated blocks, and premium channels, in addition to the three major networks established in the early days of radio.

Sponsorship Patterns

In the earliest days of radio and television, children's programs were often supported on a sustaining basis but, as stated earlier, as children became identified as having some expendable income or influence on family purchases, advertisers were willing to buy time as they did for adult program-ming. Initially, programs that were nationally distributed would often have single sponsors, such as Anacin's *Junior Nurse Corps* or Hecker Cereal's sponsorship of *Bobby Benson*. There are still rare occasions when this occurs, as with Ronald McDonald's *Family Theater*. When there were single sponsor-ships, programs and products had a clear association, such as *Little Orphan Annie* and Ovaltine or *Jack Armstrong, All American Boy* and Wheaties. With television's rising production costs, increased competition, and the growth of profit poten-tial from advertising time, sponsorship forms changed as attempts were made to compensate.[9]

Prior to 1980, arrangements between the toy and media industries were made where, for a fee and a percentage of the profits, the name and image of a media personality was licensed to a manufacturing company. These companies, in turn, produced consumer goods using the likeness of the media characters. The lines separating producer and creator were clear. There have been a few notable exceptions to these arrangements: *The Monkees,* on prime-time television in 1966, and *Hot Wheels,* aired on Saturday morning in 1969. The Monkees were a musical group of four young men selected for their marketability rather than their singing ability. They were heavily marketed to the preteen audience on television, in the recording industry, and on T-shirts, lunch boxes, and other paraphernalia. Although the group was very popular and presented respectable ratings on television, they did not generate a trend of merchandise licensing and programming. In 1969, Mattel toy company introduced a television program based on a line of their Hot Wheels toy cars. But, like the Monkees, the program did not establish a trend. The climate of government regulation policy and the limited channels of distribution discouraged further development of these types of arrangements. It was with the increased demand for pro-grams and a change in regulatory climate that relationships shifted and media stars became product characters. Or is it that product characters became media stars?

In Fall 1980, when the *Smurfs* was introduced on Saturday morning, there was an environment receptive to more innovative financial arrangements. In 1994, when Mattel brought back a version of the *Hot Wheels* program, no one commented. The *Smurfs* simultaneous success on Saturday morning television and in the marketplace is used here to mark the beginning of this new genre—they were followed quickly by *Strawberry Shortcake, Care Bears, G.I. Joe,* and *ThunderCats.* Since then, each television season has seen the introduction of programming linked with the toy industry. The motion picture industry entered the arena with an increasing number of animated movies for the young audience, all with marketable items and product endorsements that are either tie-ins or coproductions (Wasko, Phillips, & Purdie, 1993). This author's favorite is the Little Mermaid plastic aquarium, complete except for fish.

A number of economic and political factors were at work in the 1980s that were not in place in 1966 or in 1969, when *The Monkees* and Mattel's *Hot Wheels* were introduced. For example, in the intervening years, children had become an increasing target in the consumer market and were lavished with an unprecedented array of consumer goods. A climate of deregulation allowed the marketplace to determine the definition of children's programming—based on economics, not public interest; the toy industry began aggressive marketing, and the rising cost of television production made outside investments a necessity. Although some of these factors might have been in place in the 1960s, it was the combination of events that prompted change.

However, it must be noted that any changes in sponsorship patterns have been of "degree" not "substance." The children's radio industry established the norms of sponsorship and programming. General Mills, then as now, was one of the major advertisers to children. From 1930 to 1951, about 50% of the programs were fully sponsored by the major cereal companies, about 20% were fully sponsored by some other product affiliation (e.g., the House of Books' *Story Hour* and Anacin's *Junior Nurse Corps*), and about 20% were supported on a sustaining basis (Summers, 1971). Except for brief periods when children's programming was supported by the broadcast industry as it attempted to sell itself to the public, most of children's programming has been commercially sponsored. It is the economic arrangements among the advertisers, producers, distributors, and stations that have changed.

Other economic decisions that, at first, appear to have nothing to do with children have also influenced the new relationship of toys and television. In the 1980s, advertiser-supported programming, programming bartered to the stations for advertising time, became an important part of the market. Stations no longer had to put up capital to buy programming. In some instances, there were links between the program production company, the advertiser, and the barter agent. For example, an agent for a toy company could receive X minutes of advertising time on a station in exchange for a program produced by a production house with links to the toy company. Economic investments were spread between advertiser, television station, program production companies, and toy manufacturer.

The next chapter will examine the consequences of barter and syndication on the relationship between advertisers and television stations. Production and sponsorship came together as the demand for programming, a result of the Federal Communications Commission rulings, created an environment where the toy companies could enter into the business of children's television.

3
♦♦♦

The Industries:
Television and Toy

In part, the development of a children's consumer culture centers around the desire to generate profit and spread economic risk in two financially volatile industries—entertainment and leisure. Because of the difficulty in predicting success, these industries are particularly sensitive to the whims of the marketplace; although television is subject to the regulatory authority of government, the industry is still driven by the need to generate profits.

Economic imperatives that have shaped the current relationship between the entertainment and leisure industries include, for example, competition for programming and advertising time in the television industry, and attempts to stabilize the high-risk toy industry. Over time, these two industries have come together in a symbiotic relationship that blurs the lines between program and product. On television, programs offer the toy-industry advertisements for characters, and the toys present the entertainment industry with readily identifiable characters.

To place these, and the child as consumer/audience, in a corporate context, this chapter will include a brief history of the two industries. The first section will focus on the independent television stations, because they have been the primary source of toy or character-based programming. The second section will explore developments in the toy industry that also contributed to children's entertainment. Both lead to the child as an audience segment and consumer market.

The story begins with an account of the television industry's growth[1] and events that led to that growth: a competitive programming and advertising market, readily available advertiser-supported programming, and an expanding syndication market.

THE TELEVISION INDUSTRY

Prior to 1976, many of the programs on the few existing independent stations were game shows, off-network reruns, old theatrical cartoons, and B-movies. But several events occurred in the mid-1970s that contributed to the expansion of television. These events were varied and included, but were not limited to, first, the Federal Communications Commission's (FCC's) Prime-Time Access Rule (PTAR) and the Financial and Syndication Rulings (Fin-Syn) that expanded the market for independent productions, and second, an increased demand for advertising time (Frazier Gross & Kadlec Inc., 1986) which eventually led to an increased demand for children's programming.

For the television industry, as discussed in earlier chapters, it is important to consider both government and economic forces when discussing change. Regulation such as PTAR and Fin-Syn can have an effect on the marketplace, though sometimes unintended. Here, the focus is on the economic forces that drive decision making in the industry.

For example, in 1969, it was a toy competitor of Mattel, not concerned citizens, that brought a claim against the ABC network when it was airing the television program *Hot Wheels*. Topper Corporation charged that *Hot Wheels* was nothing more than a 30-minute commercial for Mattel's Hot Wheels toys. The FCC ruled that some parts of the program could be considered as commercial time and expressed concern with this "disturbing pattern" (Federal Communications Commission, 1984). ABC dropped the program. But a second look at what appears to be the network conceding to an FCC ruling could also be an economic decision ("Hot Wheels Doesn't Push," 1970). No matter what the FCC had ruled in the *Hot Wheels* case, it was a buyer's market for children's programming. So, ABC could, as they did, drop the program and replace it with a less controversial program. In the 1980s, in part because of an increase in the number of television stations that was an unintended consequence of PTAR, it was a seller's market, with a heavy demand for children's programming. Anything that could fill a half-hour was bought, including the kind of programming that previously showed the "disturbing pattern" of commercialism, toy-based programming.

All through the 1970s, there were hearings before the FCC on behalf of the children (FCC docket 19142) that brought only minor changes in children's programming; on the other hand, the PTAR and Fin-Syn rulings were instrumental in forming new markets to be filled with first-run, advertiser-supported programming—this did bring about change in the children's television industry. These rulings brought about structural change to the television industry by increasing the number of new, independent television stations and a need for programming to fill on-air hours. This profusion of poorly capitalized independents presented a unique environment to bring together the child consumer and audience. Advertiser-supported children's shows were a welcome source of programming hours for the independents.

The number of independent stations available in the United States increased from 85 stations in 1976 to 226 stations in 1985, and 443 stations in 1993 (*Revolution*, 1985; Grillo, 1988; "Year in Review," 1994). By comparison, the number of network-affiliated television stations had only increased from 560 stations in 1974 to 630 stations in 1984, and has remained relatively constant (*Revolution*, 1985; "Year in Review," 1994).

Prior to 1977, the independent stations were primarily found in the major markets and could claim barely 10% of the viewing audience. This limitation on audience size, of course, limited the station's access to advertiser dollars and attractive programming, but the growth in stations created a demand for programming hours. For example, in 1975, independent stations needed 10,374 hours of programming to fill on-air time; by 1984, the number of programming hours required to cover the new stations rose to 28,400 hours (*Revolution*, 1985). The demand for programming among affiliated or network-owned stations experienced a minimal increase: from 25,200 hours in 1975 to 28,400 hours in 1984 (*Revolution*, 1985). Much of the demand on independent stations was for children's programs, whereas children's programming on the networks remained relatively constant or declined.

Thus, a strengthening of available programming, the growth in advertising demand, an increase in barter arrangements, and a restructuring of the syndicated programming market contributed to the independent stations position as competition for network advertising revenue.

Programming

As a result of the structural changes brought about by PTAR, independent stations were able to use strong syndicated programming to develop a lead-in to their prime-time hours. Using popular off-network programs such as *M*A*S*H* and *All in the Family,* independents were able to attract an audience and demonstrate their potential as viable advertising markets. Between fall 1975 and fall 1976, audience shares in nine of the major television markets increased substantially ("Indies Get Sizable Shares," 1978). So, a cycle was begun—the larger the audience shares, the better the advertising revenues, the more stations enter the market, the greater the need for programming, the larger audience shares. What served to strengthen the adult market for the independents also worked to strengthen the children's market.

Advertising Time

The second factor that accounted for the growth of independent stations was the reduction in available network advertising time in the late 1970s and early 1980s, forcing advertisers to look elsewhere.

> Nineteen seventy-six was a watershed year in tv. Money seemingly dropping from the skies as the Olympics and presidential election—aided and abetted by those 30 minutes a night less of prime time on the nets from PTAR—forced prices up and availabilities to disappear. The 25-year-old business grew an astonishing 100% in revenue; the indies grew even more. (Block, 1988, p. 77)

Because high-demand programming such as the Olympics and the presidential election filled many of the available advertising hours during the mid-1970s, network advertising time sold out early. This resulted in a need for substitute outlets. In addition, this shortage of advertising time encouraged networks to increase prices to advertisers. Advertisers, faced with limited availability and spiraling costs, turned to alternative markets such as independent stations (Lorimar/Telepictures, 1985). This further strengthened the independents' position in the television industry.

Barter Sales

The third factor that contributed to the growth of independent television stations was the success of cash/barter arrangements. Independent stations, particularly small-market stations, are traditionally low-budget operations with minimal capitalization. Therefore, they rely heavily on creative financial arrangements such as advertiser-supported programming as an alternative way of financing program acquisition. The growth of barter paralleled the growth of independent stations. Programming costs can account for more than one-half an independent station's operation expenses and, if these costs are covered by advertiser-supported programming, stations are able to work with much lower capitalization. This was extremely important to many of the independent stations that had invested heavily in acquisition and capital development during the late 1970s and early 1980s, leaving little money for programming.

Advertiser-supported programming offered these stations economic viability. Stations with limited resources could trade advertising time for first-run, syndicated programs. In 1973, there were only 31 bartered programs filling independents' daytime hours with programs such as *Celebrity Bowling* and *Living Easy with Dr. Joyce Brothers* (Forkan, 1973).

It is important to note that the actual percentage of barter hours *per station* did not increase significantly—the average number of barter-hours stayed relatively constant on affiliates (7–8%) and independents (23–29%). However, the number of advertiser dollars rose as a consequence of the *increased number of stations* (Butterfield Communications Group, 1986) that now had more programs from which to choose.

These creative financial arrangements, designed to meet stations' programming needs and the need for advertising time, coupled with the escalating cost of program production, contributed to the demand for barter agreements. The success of bartering can be attributed to the independent stations' demand for program hours and the opportunity for advertisers and program producers to assure programming costs would be covered.

Syndicated Programming

The fourth contribution to the growth of independent stations was the restructuring of the syndication market. In part, this restructuring can be attributed to the changing programming philosophy at the networks about this time, the late 1970s and early 1980s. Generally, when a program is canceled after one season, too few episodes have been produced to put the program into syndication. The competitive programming environment of 1976 led to frequent cancellations and a short supply of network, prime-time programming for eventual off-network syndication (Lorimar/Telepictures, 1985). This scarcity of supply was offset by the growing, first-run syndication market. First-run syndication programs are financed by a variety of agents (producers, distributors, stations, advertisers, advertising agencies, or any combination thereof) and generally packaged as barter arrangements. Where once undercapitalized stations, and especially small stations, had to be satisfied with low-cost, off-network reruns or yet another game show, now they had access to more competitive programming: *PM Magazine, Donahue,* and *Oprah,* or *She's the Sheriff;* and, important to this discussion, cartoons such as *He-Man and the Masters of the Universe, Rainbow Brite, Smoggies, Widget, Goof Troop,* and *Twinkle.*

First-run programming was now available to independent stations with a minimal investment of cash, using the more readily negotiable commercial airtime. A number of industry observers credit the increased demand for advertiser-supported, first-run, syndicated programs to the proliferation of independent stations (see, e.g., McGann & Russell, 1981; MacGregor, 1984; *Revolution,* 1985; Brown, 1986).

Much of that demand, then as now, has been for children's programming. While the television industry was expanding and production companies were seeking alternative (creative) ways to finance the new television programs, there were changes happening in the toy industry that offered interesting possibilities.

THE TOY INDUSTRY

The toy industry is among the oldest manufacturing industries in the United States, but it has always been a very capricious business. Changing demographics, the seasonal nature of the industry, and the high-risk investments involved in production contribute to its instability (Stern & Schoenhaus, 1990). Events in the industry during the 1970s and 1980s encouraged economic stabilization by (1) consolidating the market, (2) encouraging year-round sales, and (3) reducing the high, up-front risk of production costs. Santa Claus becomes cost-efficient.

The nation's birthrate (fewer babies/fewer toys), expendable household income, and even family structure, contribute to the toy industry's volatile nature. For example, demographic changes, such as older parents or longevity, indicate more expendable family income or more grandparents to buy more "things." An increase in the divorce rate means more households and more places to have toys. Small increases or decreases in the birthrate can impact significantly on the toy business, as can shifts in salaries and wages—among the first to go in a tight money market are leisure purchases such as toys.

Until the 1970s, up to 80% of toy sales were in the six weeks before Christmas ("Toys and Television," 1956; Owen, 1986). Toy purchases were the responsibility of adults: Advertising, sales, and production were all geared to fourth-quarter holiday sales to parents, grandparents, aunts and uncles, and Santa Claus. Although the market still relies heavily on fourth-quarter sales, there has been an important shift to year-round marketing. As children acquired their own disposable income and influenced family spending, year-round marketing became feasible.

Successful toy sales are also dependent on anticipating the whim of 5-year-olds (or their parents), 18 months in advance— what the 5-year-olds of then, not the 5-year-olds of now, will be talking about on the playground. Development, production, and distribution costs are high in an industry where there are only a few hot items per season. Although character licensing eliminates much of the risk, many decisions are still based on "gut instinct" or "low cost intuition" (*Sales Growth Slowed*, 1986). Consequently five of the major toy companies, and a television network, rejected one of the most successful toys of the decade—the *Cabbage Patch Kids* ("NBC Fumbles," 1983; *Sales Growth Slowed*, 1986).

Some attempts to bring product stability to the toy industry include increasing the use of market research and research and development departments, and subcontracting production to foreign facilities. Other strategies of risk management that have particular consequences here involve extending the life cycle of a product and shifting the emphasis from generic toy to licensed paraphernalia using television programs, videocassettes, storybooks and comic books, and commercials.

Market Consolidation

By observing changes in the toy industry, the use of corporate expansion and acquisition, and product diversification to strengthen the market becomes apparent. Each strategy serves to reinforce the corporate structure and minimize the risk of new toy ventures.

To begin, the industry became increasingly concentrated, starting with a flurry of mergers in the early 1980s: Hasbro merged with Milton Bradley; Hallmark acquired Binney Smith; and the CBS broadcasting network purchased Ideal Toys (Standard & Poor Industry Trends, 1984). The Hasbro–Bradley merger brought advantages to each company: Hasbro gained access to Bradley's successful international market, and Bradley gained the domestic licensing rights to Hasbro characters such as My Little Pony, G.I. Joe, and Transformers; board games using the My Little Pony and G.I. Joe characters were featured at the following year's Toy Fair ("Hasbro's Urge," 1985). In 1985, Kenner Parker was spun off as an independent company by its parent corporation, General Mills; in 1987, it was acquired by Tonka Corporation, bringing together three of the larger American toy companies—Kenner Parker Toys, Parker Brothers, and Tonka (Stern, 1987; "Tonka to Acquire," 1987). In 1991, Hasbro acquired Tonka (U.S. Department of Commerce, 1992).

In 1980, the top three toymakers (Hasbro, Mattel, and Coleco) shared about 20% of the market; by 1985, they controlled close to 35% ("Battle of the Fun Factories", 1985); in 1986, the top five toymakers (Kenner Parker Toys, Fisher–Price, Hasbro, Mattel, Coleco Industries) controlled 45% of a market that includes about 700 firms (Owen, 1986); in 1990, the 10 largest companies controlled 60% of the market (Stern & Schoenhaus, 1990). By 1992, the market was dominated by five or six companies (Clout, 1992). (In 1996, Mattel made an unsuccessful attempt to purchase Hasbro, which would have closed the market.)

Coleco as a Case Study

Economic stability through acquisition and merger can be demonstrated by changes in corporate structure at Coleco. Initially, the company was a single-product corporation, vulnerable to the whim of a fad. In 1982, 73% of its investments were in electronic games; in 1985, 77% of the business was invested in Cabbage Patch Kids. The company spent 1986 in a series of acquisitions that strengthened its position in other categories of the toy industry, such as board games and collectible figures (Coleco Industries, Inc., 1986). According to the 1986 Annual Report, "the achievement of this strategic objective has brought much needed breadth and balance to Coleco's product line, strengthening our ability to compete successfully and providing the foundation for future growth and stability" (p. 3). Unfortunately, this was not enough to overcome the caprice of the toy industry. With the waning popularity of the Cabbage Patch Dolls, Coleco found it necessary to file for Chapter 11, protection from bankruptcy. However, the strategy has been successful for other companies such as Mattel and Hasbro.

Year-Round Marketing

In addition to mergers and acquisitions, an important protective strategy in the toy industry has been the move to year-round sales. In 1970 Ruth Handler, cofounder of Mattel, said:

> The most important ways in which toy manufacturers, as well as wholesalers and retailers, can mutually enhance their profit performances, can be summed up in two words: seasonality and communications.
>
> Any steps taken that reduce the seasonal peaks and raise the seasonal valleys—be those steps in the form of product design, or product introduction timing, or promotion and merchandising programming benefit the entire industry. ("Mattel's Handlers," 1970)

Television's influence on advertising patterns certainly contributed to changes in the seasonality of the toy market. With Mattel's advertisements on *The Mickey Mouse Club* came a rethinking of the consumer market "from customer driven, where the customer decided what he wanted, to being a consumer-communication business" (Loomis, cited in Owen, 1986), that is, telling the consumer what he or she should want. And the Saturday morning children's programs served the intent of being "consumer-communication" quite well. Toy manufacturers could adopt a year-round, rather than a seasonal, advertising schedule, using television to reach the child consumer. No longer did the consumer go to the toy store only when a product was needed for a particular event such as Christmas or a birthday. Now the cornucopia of toys was brought to the living room each Saturday morning or weekday afternoon.

Yet another factor contributing to the year-round sale of toys is the increased availability of "collectibles," small toys primarily designed to accumulate—the Smurfs included 100 collectible figurines representing each of the 99 Smurfs, Smurfette, Papa Smurf, and various babies. In a previous chapter the attraction of collecting to a young child was discussed. As early as 1935, Grumbine pointed out that children show a strong interest in collecting. Then she talked in terms of stamps and coins and rocks; now, the "things" children collect are often merchandise products. It would take many birthdays and holidays for a little girl to collect all the bits to the Rainbow Brite, Care Bears, or Smurfs. And the Teenage Mutant Ninja Turtles offer a remarkable range of villains and heroes. Toys, no longer presents or surprises, have become staples in a consumer market.

Perhaps one of the most important events in the move toward year-round availability has been the development of large-volume toy stores. These stores have provided a wider retail range year-round than was previously available. Prior to megastores such as Toys 'R' Us and Child World, the seasonality of the market was reinforced by the difficulty in locating well-stocked shelves during times other than Christmas. Toys were stocked by department, discount, and variety stores in seasonal sections. Toys 'R' Us radically changed the process. The company first appeared as a nationwide supermarket of toys in 1966. From 1975 to 1985, annual revenues grew from $200 million to $2 billion, and 1992 sales were estimated at $7.2 billion (Owen, 1986; Clout, 1992). Much of the company's success can be attributed to the fact that it serves as a year-round outlet for toy sales: Most of the Toys 'R' Us stores offer more than 16,000 different toys, 352 days per year. As of 1994, there were 581 stores in the United States and 234 international stores in 70 foreign markets ("Toys 'R' Us Announces," 1994).

Risk Management

It is difficult to control a market as unstable as the toy industry, but altering the industry structure through market consolidation and introducing year-round sales to change consumer buying habits has served to bring some measure of economic balance. In addition, the toy industry has introduced several strategies to control risk that are central to the children's media market. These strategies for risk management are based on product stability, brought about by extending the life cycle of existing products and shifting the emphasis from generic toy to licensed product.

Extended Shelf Life

Traditionally the toy industry has been considered "fad bound"; that is, products appear and disappear sometimes with no reasonable explanation—witness the Hula Hoop. Manufacturers have discovered that by linking toys to television, the longevity of a product line can be enhanced. For example, Smurf toys and television shows have been available for almost 15 years, thus entertaining a third and fourth generation of viewers. And although their popularity (and sales) have declined, the Smurf cartoons are still offered as off-network syndication in many markets and as a staple on the Cartoon Cable Channel and Toys 'R' Us still carries a limited range of Smurf toys.

As network cartoon programs go into syndication or are reissued, there is a renewed interest in the toy. Adding new characters to a line also revives interest in the product, something that cannot be done easily with a single-item product such as Raggedy Ann. A chronology of the *Care Bears* offers an interesting example of the use of media, product licensing, and market savvy to extend the life of a character.[2]

1982: Care Bears are introduced for Spring 1983 as toys, licensed characters (25 licensees preproduction), and media stars. Based on characters developed jointly by Those Characters from Cleveland (licensing division of American Greetings) and M.A.D. (Marketing and Design Service of the toy group of General Mills), the initial series of bears include Cheer Bear, Friend Bear, Tender-Heart Bear, Birthday Bear, Grumpy Bear, Funshine Bear, Good Luck Bear, Wish Bear, and Love-A-Lot Bear.

1983: Care Bears are introduced at the Toy Fair and a television special is available for first-run syndication produced and sponsored by Kenner toy company.

1984: Care Bears television miniseries is distributed by Lexington Broadcast Services and a second line of toys—Care Bear Cousins—is issued.

1985: The Care Bears Movie is released; Care Bears family cold-care guide is available as a tie-in with the purchase of a major children's cold remedy.

1986: Care Bears Movie II is released and includes Care Bears, Care Bear Cousins, Care Bear Cubs, Care Bear Cousin Cubs. According to one reviewer, nearly every collectible is mentioned in the first 20 minutes.

1987: The Care Bears Adventure in Wonderland is released with department store tie-ins, appearances of Care Bears at daycare centers, hospitals, parades, radio stations; the Bears move to ABC-TV Saturday morning.

1988: available in off-network syndication.

1992: available on toy shelves, off-network syndication, and videocassette rental; 40 new licensees.

1994: all of the above, including regularly scheduled programming on the Disney Channel.

The product began in 1983, with its initial introduction of nine characters—each a stuffed bear toy, plus 25 licensed items such as pajamas and bed sheets. Point-of-sale interest in the stores and a television special generated demand; in 1984, the characters were again on television, attracting those too young the year before and introducing a new line of characters to the collection; with the movie in 1985, interest was sustained. In addition, every drugstore the author patronized during the flu and cold season had a large display featuring the Care Bears promoting a popular children's cough remedy. By 1986, another movie, another generation of viewers/consumers, and another line of collectibles had appeared; 1987 brought a rerelease of the movie, with local appearances of the Bears reminiscent of Bobby Benson from early radio; in 1988, the cycle repeats itself as the characters return to television. In 1996, the program is a regular part of the Disney Channel's morning lineup.

Thus, a character introduced in 1982 has a viable shelf life for over 10 years. Before television, this longevity was limited to a privileged few, such as Raggedy Ann, the teddy bear, and Barbie. With television, the cycle can be repeated as programs go into syndication or as movies are rereleased. And videocassettes are ubiquitous.

Licensed Products

One of the most significant changes in the toy industry has been the number of characters available. Another method of coping with the uncertainties of the toy business has been the development of lines of products rather than individual toys. This has been achieved through the introduction of multiple character lines and "accessorizing." No longer do the toy companies introduce generic dolls—now the Muppets have babies and Care Bears have cousins and Rainbow Brite comes with seven companions, each with its own sprite (Buddy Blue and Champ, LaLa Orange and O. J., Shy Violet and I. Q., Red Butler and Romeo, Canary Yellow and Spark, Indigo and Hammy, Patty O'Green and Lucky—then, there is Murky Dismal and Starlite Horse).[3] There are no simple Raggedy Ann or Shirley Temple dolls but rather the Get-A-Long Gang, or Millions of Unusual Small Creatures Lurking Everywhere (M.U.S.C.L.E.s), or Masters of the Universe. Accessories range from comb and brush sets for My Little Pony, environmental modules for He-Man, or power cars and wedding cakes for Barbie.

As with the Care Bears, new lines of characters begat others, and each is valuable for the right to use its image on sheets, shoes, towels, and cereal boxes which, of course, means lots of things to buy and sell. The process was described well in a high-quality, high-visibility advertisement placed in several media and merchandising trade magazines.[4] The ad ("Care Bears: Advertisement," 1984) stated:

Success runs in our family.

Only a few short years ago two very special companies put their heads and hearts together and came up with the biggest, most lovable idea in licensing history.

Us. The Care Bears.™

And since then we've put smiles on the faces of millions of kids and adults alike. Not to mention retailers.

Well, hold on to your hearts, 'cause we're ready to help you share a whole new family of feelings . . .

Meet the Care Bear Cousins . . .

Each Care Bear Cousin has its very own heart-shaped tummy symbol that tells you what its job is.

But you won't need anyone to tell you that they're going to set the hearts of America beating.

'Specially next Spring when they make their public debut in a full length, animated feature film.

It's a multi-million dollar movie starring us, the Care Bears, and the Care Bear Cousins.

The Care Bear Cousins will also be stars of the media as they join the Care Bears in 35 million dollars worth of advertising and millions more in special promotions throughout the year.

The Care Bears Cousins are going to capture the hearts of America with their own unique world of adorable Care Bear Cousin products.

But the Care Bears have quite a few exciting surprises in store for you, too.

There are new licensees. New products. New promotions. New designs.

And three new additions to our growing family: Share Bear™, Secret Bear™ and Champ Bear™. So come grow with us.

'Cause together the Care Bears and the Care Bear Cousins will show you just what you can accomplish when your heart is in the right place.

Although the concept of licensing has been around for over 100 years, and Disney established a licensing unit upon the initial success of Mickey Mouse in the 1930s, it was in the late 1970s that licensing gained popularity and legitimacy. Until the early 1980s, most agreements were between creators or media producers to use a character for product manufacturing. Walt Disney's licensing unit, Retlaw, allowed clothing manufacturers to make sweatshirts with the image of Mickey Mouse for a royalty fee. However, since 1980, there have been new configurations, like the Care Bears, designed as a character property with no prior history. Constructed from the imagination of those at American Greetings, a greeting-card manufacturer, the original ten Bears (Cheer Bear, Friend Bear, Tender-Heart Bear, Birthday Bear, Grumpy Bear, Bedtime Bear, Funshine Bear, Good Luck Bear, Wish Bear, and Love-A-Lot Bear) were proposed primarily as character properties to be licensed to others ("American Greetings," 1982). The strategic release of television specials, book promotions, and movies extended the shelf life of retail goods, and the licensed products brought familiarity to the merchandise.

THE LICENSING INDUSTRY

Character licensing is an agreement that allows the right to use a name or image in exchange for a royalty fee (generally 5–15% of the wholesale cost of an item). Institutions and corporations profit from these arrangements through the licensing of their emblems and symbols. Nowadays, this is evident in the number of baseball hats and jackets that carry the imprint of college or professional sports team and T-shirts that feature product icons. The goals of character or product licensing have been to increase name recognition, create a secondary income source, and protect trade names from illegal use (Kesler, 1987). Such arrangements benefit the entertainment business with new investment capital for production, product visibility and demand, and advertisement revenue. Benefits to the manufacturing company include readily identifiable characters and "free" advertisements. Increasingly, licensing fees are also an important source of corporate revenue and agents are hired to arrange contractual agreements for the use of a name or image.

While sports teams and products such as Coca-Cola and Pepsi have become involved in licensing their corporate names and symbols, among the most successful retail areas involved in licensing has been the toy industry.

Opponents of the phenomenon have claimed it is simply a license to steal: One comes up with a cute character, gives it a name and personality, and then waits for the royalty payments to arrive. Certainly, that is a simplistic, and some would say smug, representation of the process, but it is nonetheless the "philosophical" foundation to licensing. Anecdotes that support the success of licensing abound.

> Between 1933 and 1935, more than 2.5 million watches with the licensed Mickey Mouse character were sold (Upton, 1985).
>
> In the 1950s, the merchandising of Roy Rogers's Double RR brand had an annual volume of over $30 million (Gilbert, 1957).
>
> In 1954, within 6 months of the introduction of *Davy Crockett*, $100 million worth of coonskin caps were sold (Schneider, 1987).
>
> In 1974, over 300 licensed products for the *Planet of the Apes* would gross an estimated $100 million within 2 years (Forkan, 1974).

Figure 3.1 demonstrates the rapid growth in the sales of licensed products.

Income figures from the licensing industry were not kept prior to 1977, but by then it was a $4.9 billion industry (the year *Star Wars* was released), climbing to $9.9 billion in 1980 (the year of *Strawberry Shortcake*), increasing by $60 billion dollars in the 10 years between 1980 and 1990. Throughout the 1990s, figures appear to have leveled off or increased slightly, with most growth attributed to inflation rates (*Licensing Letter*, 1991; Mayer, 1992; Liebeck, 1994; Roman, 1996).

For the toy industry, the licensing concept contributed to the profitability of a toy in a number of ways: Licensed characters offer an easily identifiable toy or story line, a series of accessories or collectible items, and, through royalties, a secondary source of income. In a market that generates thousands of new items per year, the "extra income" from royalties can very important. In the mid-1970s, Hanna–Barbera, the major animation house, was grossing $40–50 million from its licensed products alone (Hanna–Barbera's tv folks, 1976), and income from royalty fees for Mattel amounted to $10 million in 1985 ("Top 100 Markets," 1986; Mattel, 1986).

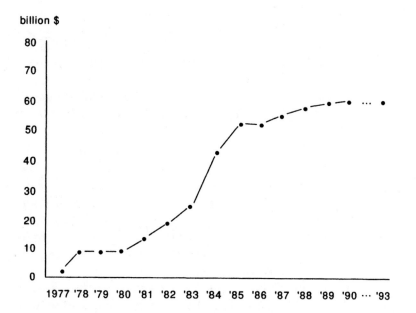

billion $

FIGURE 3.1. Sale of licensed products (in billions of dollars), 1977-1993. *Source: Licensing Letter* (1991), Inc. Data compiled from Liebeck (1994).

The growing popularity of licensed products is evident in changes to the retail market as well as the growth of licensing. In 1982, half of all toys introduced at the annual Toy Fair were associated with a licensed character (Reysen, 1982). In 1984 the sale of licensed toy products equaled more than all toy sales in 1978 (Forkan, 1985). By 1985, character licensing was 40–50% of the toy business (Forkan, 1986), and 2 years later, these products accounted for 80% of the toy business (Schneider, 1987). The 1990 Toy Fair featured tie-ins with movies (*Batman* and *Dick Tracy*), television (among others, *Teenage Mutant Ninja Turtles*), and "reality" (Matchbox's Real Model Collection, featuring Christie Brinkley, Beverly Johnson, and Cheryl Tiegs—top fashion models of the day; Harrington, 1990).

Mattel has been among the most aggressive of the toy companies in licensing arrangements with media companies. Within 1 year, the company signed the following agreements:

> April 1991: LucasArts for toys based on unspecified general and film-related concepts
> June 1991: *American Gladiators* action figures
> November 1991: Walt Disney preschool and infant toys, Disney theme-park sponsor, Hanna–Barbera Productions for plush and other toys
> December 1991: Fox TV for *Beverly Hills, 90210* toys
> January 1992: Nickelodeon activity toys (Fitzgerald, 1992)

Just as media events can expand the life of a toy, licensing can extend the popularity of television characters and keep alive a movie. A Care Bear doll is a memory of a Care Bears movie. As explained by an executive at Hanna–Barbera, "Character merchandise is not only a way to produce revenue by selling goods but it is also a very definite way of continuing the life of the character beyond the span of the television program" ("Character Licensing," 1970, p. 51).

By extending the life cycle of a character, the industries contribute to the stabilization of the toy industry and serve to ameliorate costs for the media industry—upfront investment costs are less risky if there are guarantees of longevity.

It becomes difficult to sort out production genealogies as Care Bears and Dino Riders are made movie or television stars before they are off the production line. Some "births" are quite clear: ThunderCats, He-Man, and She-Ra were joint ventures between toy and media production companies. For others the lineage is not so obvious. Q*Bert and Rubik were successful toys before they became television stars. In all cases, the intentions of those involved in production, toy or media, are self-evident. The shelf life of a successful character is extended for the toy industry and the media gains a star.

A number of events came together in the late 1970s—the desire for new markets by independent program producers ⟶ the tight advertising market and need for additional outlets ⟶ the availability of independent stations to serve as that market ⟶ the need of independent stations for programming ⟵ the growing market of young consumers ⟷ and the increasing complexities of both industries.[5] These events contributed to the shape of the current children's entertainment industry. Creative projects are the result of marketing strategies and children's imagination is tied into the market economy. Programming evolves not from the rituals of storytelling but rather the imperative of the marketplace.

4

♦♦♦

Case Studies: Smurfs and He-Man and ThunderCats

One of the consequences of the arrangements between the leisure and entertainment industries has been economic stability for the industries and a material culture for children. Mutually beneficial arrangements bring about a culture of play driven by characters available at Toys 'R' Us, not creative imagination.

The significance of an increasingly concentrated market will become evident as the genealogies of three characters that were "firsts" in the business of children's entertainment are examined. These will be discussed as markers in a changing economy. For example, the success of the Smurfs as a toy and television program encouraged the production of *He-Man and the Masters of the Universe,* a coproduction between a toy company and a production house, that encouraged the production of *ThunderCats* by a character licensing agent and television production house.

The events to be discussed are as follows:

The introduction of the Smurf toy (1979) and the *Smurf* cartoon (1981), and their symbiotic success that led those in the industry to see new marketing possibilities.[1]

The introduction of He-Man (1983) as the first event that was truly designed as toy/television, *He-Man and the Masters of the Universe* was introduced as a coproduction by Mattel toy company and Filmation production house.

The introduction of *ThunderCats* (1985), which extended the idea of product-based programming by their corporate birth at a meeting between Leisure Concepts, Inc. (a licensing agent), Telepictures (a syndication house), and Rankin-Bass (a production house).

The evolution of these mutually beneficial arrangements was inevitable in a competitive, increasingly deregulated, profit-oriented market. The number of product-based programs jumped from zero in 1980, to 14 in 1982, to 40 in 1984 (Wilke, 1985); and, although the number fluctuates from season to season, such arrangements have become a well-established part of children's entertainment. Because of the success of the Smurfs, neither toy nor story is now considered without thought of its market potential.

It is not unusual for large corporations to have in-house licensing agencies, or for toy companies to retain copyrights for their character lines. Walt Disney was among the first to see the advantages of licensing media properties when, in the late 1930s, he set up Retlaw. Mattel also has long had a policy to retain licensing rights to their toy products. Recent arrangements involve more aggressive relationships between the industries.

In 1980, the lines between organizations were clear. When working together, production companies and toy companies had contractual arrangements. By 1983, these lines were more complex and in some cases nonexistent. An analysis of the changes from the *Smurfs* to the *ThunderCats* will serve to demonstrate the shifts in and between these industries. These events will be discussed in terms of Melody's model of competition and the corporate genealogy of the companies involved (Melody, 1973).

MODELS OF UNDERSTANDING

Before beginning a discussion of the individual experiences, it is important to place these changes in the overall context of the television industry. Here, we turn to Melody's model of market exchange to explain the relationship of supply and demand as it existed in a system dominated by the networks. In 1973, he argued for a model that placed the media industries on the supply side and advertisers on the demand side. "Audience" was the commodity.

Simply put, the business of children's television, like adult programming, was driven by the principle that advertisers demand an audience of consumers, and that audience is supplied by the television or entertainment industry. An audience of merely viewers is of no value to advertisers: they must also be consumers. For example, in this model, the television stations discussed in the previous chapter serve the function of "market manager," bringing together program and audience, advertiser and consumer.[2] Advertisers purchase the time and audience that best meet the needs of the product advertiser or manufacturer. In this model, program production and distribution agents work together to supply an audience for the advertiser. Melody argued that the audience was the commodity sold to the advertiser, and his model offers an interesting starting point for this discussion. His 1973 model demonstrated a rather straightforward relationship, unencumbered by competition to the broadcasting networks. The three networks—ABC, CBS, and NBC—dominate supply side (Figure 4.1).

By 1980, other players entered the arena. The dynamics of the marketplace changed as independent stations and programming syndicators began to compete with the traditional networks for both program hours and advertising

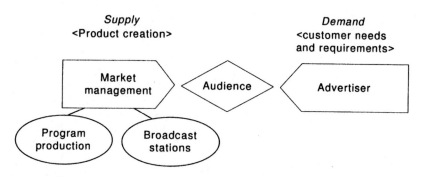

FIGURE 4.1. Market exchange in commercial broadcasting, 1973. Adapted from Melody (1973). According to Melody (1973), the broadcast networks were the primary market managers. Copyright 1973 by Yale University Press. Adapted by permission.

revenue. By 1983 (Figure 4.2), the licensing industry served as a bridge between the two agents—market managers and advertisers—serving to assure suppliers of a "known character" and advertisers with preestablished audiences. However, as we will see with the *Smurfs,* except for some syndicated specials like *Strawberry Shortcake,* these arrangements were versions of previous contractual agreements. There were no corporate ownership links or coventures.

As competition increased in the media industries (supply) and changes occurred in the toy industry (demand), the need for strong programming to attract the child audience increased. The success of characters like the Smurfs encouraged the development of similar programming. Mattel, in a joint project with Filmation, was the first to offer first-run syndicated programming as a weekly series. And, again, the dynamics shift (Figure 4.2). Here, the advertisers and licensing merchants (e.g., Mattel) moved into the supply-side of the market structure as toy companies began to promote arrangements with production houses. Contractual agreements reflect more direct involvement between manufacturer and production companies, and programs showcase toy characters (He-Man, the Care Bears, Strawberry Shortcake, or Herself the Elf).

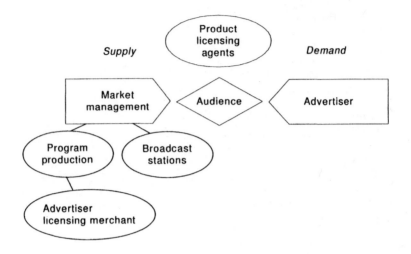

FIGURE 4.2. Market exchange in commercial broadcasting, 1983. Adapted from Melody (1973). Copyright 1973 by Yale University Press. Adapted by permission.

By 1985, the toy manufacturers moved into the area of program distribution; they not only worked to produce programs but also negotiate arrangements with broadcast stations for profit arrangements (Figure 4.3). In addition, though the model retains much the same shape as that outlined by Melody in 1973, the advertisers became more integral as they became involved in character development.

At the next stage, the relationship between market manager and product manufacturer or their representative, advertiser, became more complex as toy companies entered program production and distribution, spreading the risk that comes with the introduction of a new product. The investments of the toy companies were welcomed by the growing number of independent broadcast stations and by the new cable outlets. The marketplace shifted as product manufacturers such as toy companies played an increasing role in the production and distribution of children's entertainment.

An analysis of these three events here illustrates the growing influence of the advertiser and product manufacturer

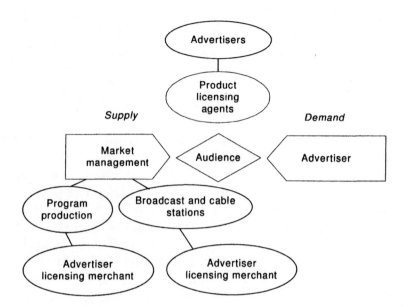

FIGURE 4.3. Market exchange in commercial broadcasting, 1985. Adapted from Melody (1973). Copyright 1973 by Yale University Press. Adapted by permission.

on children's entertainment and increasingly complex corporate relationships.

THE SMURFS

The Smurfs are little blue creatures, three apples tall, that began life in the storybooks of a Belgian author, Peyo. There are 99 characters, most identified by a trait or skill, much like Disney's seven dwarfs. In addition to the 99 characters, there was the wise Papa Smurf and the female Smurfette. The licensing rights were owned by an American novelty distributor, Wallace Berrie Company, who brought the characters from Europe. According to Hollywood legend, the Smurfs were discovered by media mogul Fred Silverman (then president of NBC), who saw the popularity of the characters among his young daughter and her friends, commissioned a cartoon series, and made the Smurfs stars ("The Selling of the Smurfs," 1982; Greene & Spragins, 1982). Introduced in the Saturday morning lineup in 1981, *Smurfs* quickly brought NBC from last to first place in the Saturday morning ratings.

As a Toy

Wallace Berrie Company was a product-licensing agent manufacturing small gifts primarily for stationery suppliers. In 1979, the company bought the rights to license the Smurf name and image in the United States from SEPP (a Belgian media firm), and within 2 years the toys were doing $600 million in retail sales (Greene & Spragins, 1982). The first products were 2-inch, soft plastic collectibles that represented the Smurf characters and sold for $1.50. These were quickly followed by key chains and plush toys, and outdoor equipment and clothing apparel, and yogurt, cereal, and record players and coloring books, and . . . It is claimed that one New Jersey family collected over 1,300 Smurfabilia items (*Smurfun*, 1983). By 1980, the year of the premiere of the Saturday morning cartoon show, there were 40 licensees, and from 1979 to 1983, sales for the company doubled each year ("How They Keep the Smurfs," 1983). An advertisement for their fifth birthday featured a partial list of 50 licensees that included Hallmark Cards, the Ice Capades, Milton Bradley, and BBC International.

Baby Smurf was introduced in 1984 (babies come along only once in a blue moon) in both the retail market and the television program, bringing a new line of toys and stories, and a renewed interest in the program. Although interest in the licensed toys waned in the late 1980s, the program is still available in syndication. The toys returned to the toy shelves of Toys 'R' Us in 1996.

The Smurfs have also shown up in our culture through references in comic strips and television programs and rap music. The Reverend Run Love of Run-DMC raps: "God is Papa Smurf and he looks down on these Smurfs. When you take two steps toward Papa Smurf, he'll take 12 steps toward you." Each legitimate use of the images brings Wallace Berrie Company a royalty payment.

As Television

NBC scheduled the *Smurfs* on Saturday mornings in 1981 and within months, it brought the network a major share of the child audience. Because of demand, NBC was able to increase up-front advertising sales by about 40% (Loftus, 1982). Four years later, the *Smurfs* were still among the top-rated Saturday morning series.

Their progress was somewhat typical of network program production. NBC had contractual arrangements with SEPP for the television rights to the character and, in a coproduction agreement, Hanna–Barbera animated the story lines. The author and creator of the *Smurfs*, Peyo, served as script consultant to Hanna–Barbera ("Move Over Snoopy," 1982). The lines were clear: SEPP owned the idea, NBC supplied the outlet, and Hanna–Barbera produced the animated program (Figure 4.4a).

When the show went into syndication in 1986, the organizational lines began to blur (Figure 4.4b). Hanna–Barbera Productions retained the syndication rights to the program with TPE as the distributor for the show ("Telerep Arm Gets,"

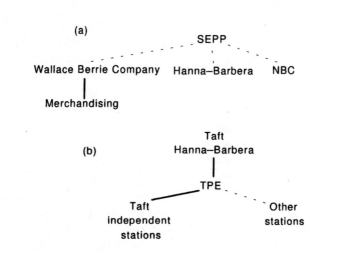

FIGURE 4.4. (a) The *Smurfs*, network programming, 1980. (b) The *Smurfs*, off-network syndication, 1986. - - - - - - - contractual links; ——————— in-house links.

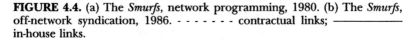

1984). At this point, contractual links, based on competition, are not clear. Connections demonstrate a more "familial" relationship. Telerep, parent company to TPE, was the national sales representatives for Taft Broadcasting, parent company of Hanna–Barbera. The Taft broadcasting stations were partners in some ventures with Cox Broadcasting, parent company to Telerep ("Telerep Arm Gets," 1984; "Tribune, Telerep Conclude," 1987). When the *Smurfs* went into syndication, independent stations owned by Taft had first right of refusal ("Smurfs Now Bartered," 1984).

But the lines between toy and program, though mutually beneficial, were clear. There was no organized attempt to spread the risk of the product's success. Wallace Berrie Company maintained the rights to merchandise and product licensing, and SEPP, NBC, and Hanna–Barbera were responsible for program production and distribution.

Corporate Structure

As the following model demonstrates, the links between toy and program production for the Smurfs were distinct.

Wallace Berrie Company owned the product merchandising rights for toys, food products, clothing and all retail goods. Hanna–Barbera (a subsidiary of Taft) maintained a coproduction agreement with SEPP for NBC. As with Melody's 1973 model, the lines of supply and demand were clear as advertisers bought time and producers made programs.

Later events were not so simple. The Smurfs' success as a licensed character and entertainment product was obvious to those in both industries. One group that built on the success of the Smurfs was the licensing division of American Greetings. The group, Those Kids From Cleveland, developed several character ideas such as Strawberry Shortcake that were sold as both programs and merchandise. These television shows were generally developed as specials or short-run series. It was the toy company, Mattel, and the production house, Filmation Studios, that put together the first weekly series based on licensed characters. The networks were nervous about potential FCC intervention and turned down programs they felt might be challenged as advertisement for toys. But *He-Man and the Masters of the Universe* was exactly what the independent stations were looking for: first-run programming, competitive with the networks, that involved minimal capitalization.

HE-MAN AND THE MASTERS OF THE UNIVERSE

Mattel introduced He-Man as a joint project with Filmation. There was no attempt to disguise the relationship; the announcement about the series was made at a press conference with the president of Filmation and the senior vice-president of marketing from Mattel ("Group W Readies," 1982); creative control remained with Mattel (Mattel, 1984). "Mattel did a lot of research before 'Masters of the Universe' was developed. We found out that what interests kids is fantasy, timelessness, and good versus evil. Based on this, we set the producers and writers to work" (Carlson, 1986, p. 57).

For the uninitiated, He-Man lives in the land of Eternia, and he does indeed offer children "fantasy, timelessness, and good versus evil." On nearby Snake Mountain lives Skeletor—evil incarnate. Every episode features a battle between He-Man (good) and Skeletor, and one of his many minions (evil). Prince Adam (He-Man's alter ego) is supported by Org, a gremlin-like character; Tella, Captain/Captainess of the Guard; and Prince Adam's twin sister, She-Ra, who later had her own series. When evil lurks, Prince Adam raises his sword and is transformed into He-Man. He is then off with his "Heroic Warriors" to do battle with Skeletor and the "Evil Warriors."

Each story is built around a moral principle, each half hour ends with a homily, and each character is sold separately.

As a Toy

He-Man was not only powerful in the land of Eternia but also in the world of market economy. In 1984, worldwide sales were estimated at $500 million; between 1982 and 1985, 125 million character dolls were sold—the equivalent of 11 to each U.S. boy between the ages of 5 and 10 (Wilke, 1985; "Top 100 Markets," 1985; "Battle of the Fun Factories," 1985). The following is a representative list of characters available within the first year from the Mattel Toy Company. Like many of the product-based characters, they are built around the principle of collectibility discussed earlier.

Heroic warriors	*Evil warriors*
Roboto	Stinkor
Moss Man	Two Bad
Sy-Klone	Whiplash
Orko	Beast Man
Buzz-Off	Spikor
Fisto	Clawful
Teela	Evil-Lyn
Mekaneck	Jitsu
Stratos	Kobra Kahn
Man-at-Arms	Webstor
Man-E-Faces	Mer-Man
Several versions of He-Man	Trap-Jaw
	Tri-Klops
	Several versions of Skeletor

New characters and new accouterments were introduced and promotional campaigns were used to build consumer awareness. One particularly creative promotion was a create-a-character contest; children were encouraged to submit character designs. After the top five drawings were selected—Fearless Photog, Netta, Compactor, Eye Beam, and Brainwave—children were invited to call in and vote for their favorite. The winner of the design selected, Fearless Photog, was a 12-year-old boy who was awarded "an actual toy made from his idea," the right to be Honorary President of Mattel for a day, and a $100,000 college scholarship. More mundane promotions included stickers in cereal boxes.

In addition to the weekly television series, there were other media events that Mattel anticipated would "stimulate renewed domestic interest in the product line," including a stage show, a live-action movie (Mattel, 1986; Dawson, 1987), and a 1986 Christmas television program replayed yearly.

As Television

The program was introduced on independent television stations in the fall of 1983. It had first been offered to the networks but was reported to have been turned down because of Mattel's involvement (Wilke, 1985; Englehardt, 1986) and the possibility the FCC would hold it to the definition of product-based programming. Nonetheless, in syndication the show covered 65 markets the first year and had 82% market coverage on independent stations by the second year (Wilke, 1985; Englehardt, 1986). To introduce the series, Mattel staged Hollywood-style premieres in 10 major U.S. cities for a feature-length movie that was, in fact, three television episodes ("Masters' Premiere," 1983).

Because of high program costs, Group W (parent company to Filmation) negotiated a 2-year commitment from stations to guarantee the cost of production ("Group W Readies," 1982). Program quality and costs were competitive with the networks' animation ("Telepictures to Pitch," 1984; Dempsey, 1984). But because of Mattel's commitment to advertising time, risk to the stations was minimized. Stations had a guaranteed commitment of advertising revenue from Mattel; Mattel, on the other hand, had up-front assurances of advertising time from the stations. Fortunately for Mattel, Filmation Studios, and the stations, *He-Man* consistently drew high ratings in the afternoon time period on independent stations.

Not only was *He-Man and the Masters of the Universe* a popular television program in the United States but it also had a worldwide audience in as many as 42 countries (Mattel, 1984). Filmation sold episodes to England, Ireland, Colombia, Venezuela, and the Caribbean ("Filmation Posts," 1986). In 1985 it was the number-one program in Germany ("Top 100 Markets," 1986).

But *He-Man and the Masters of the Universe* would be just another fantasy cartoon if it were not for the innovative arrangements that it offered the independent television stations. The success of the program as a first-run, advertiser-supported show made it the "single major factor ... for the immense new-production, kid-syndicated activity" (Sobel, 1984b, p. 34). It offered independent stations something new; no longer did the stations need to rely on the tired, off-network situation comedies as counterprogramming to the networks. The program gave the independent stations competitive strength by being both first-run and advertiser-supported (Sobel, 1983, 1984a).

Corporate Structure

From the beginning, *He-Man and the Masters of the Universe* was a united effort by Mattel and Group W Productions (parent company to Filmation). According to promotional material:

> Mattel Toys and Group W Productions are teaming up for an unusual first-run syndicated tv program, an animated tv series ...
>
> The *Masters of the Universe* line, eight separate action play figures introduced by Mattel in the spring, will be brought to TV ...
>
> Filmation, the Group W animation house, will produce and Group W Productions will syndicate *He-Man and Masters of the Universe* on a barter basis ...
>
> Mattel Toys will be a barter sponsor and, in another unusual aspect, is taking part in financing production for what is a joint venture with Group W.
>
> Each action figure toy comes with a comics [*sic*] book that describes a whole mythology (created in-house by Mattel Toys) built around controlling Castle Greyskull. ("Group W, Mattel Toys Team for TV," 1982, p. 20)

The arrangement was considered a "cofinancing" deal, with three companies splitting the costs—Mattel, Group W, and Filmation (Seligman, 1983; Jereski, 1983). There were no direct ownership links between Mattel and Group W/Filmation but each company had a vested interest in the economic success of the product. And although Mattel claimed the company did not write scripts for the program, it was reported that they could appear to "exercise creative input" reviewing scripts and making suggestions (Carlson, 1986). One result of these suggestions was Enchantra the Swan, suggested by Mattel to Filmation Studios for the *She-Ra, Princess of Power* series, adding another character to the product line, the fairy tale, and the toy shelf (Diamond, 1987).

Figure 4.5, when compared to the earlier corporate configurations of the Smurfs demonstrates the increasing linkage between the toy and program production lines.

The link between Group W and Filmation was described as "fortuitous and lucky" (as well as economically prudent) by Lou Scheimer, president of Filmation, when discussing the merger of the parent companies of Group W Productions (Westinghouse) and Filmation (Teleprompter). He was quoted as saying:

> We never had the ability, because of our parent company, to be involved in a company with a syndication arm . . . we always had to go outside, pay somebody 35% off the top to distribute our programs. . . . We're not faced with any of these problems. We have a company that can afford to finance the stuff we produce. (Gelman, 1984, p. 35)

Until *He-Man*, Filmation had produced programming exclusively for the networks. Because the show proved that first-run syndication could be a success, within 4 years, the organization stopped producing network programming to focus exclusively on the syndication market (Gelman, 1984; "Filmation Lets Go," 1987).

FIGURE 4.5. *He-Man and the Masters of the Universe,* first-run syndication, 1983. - - - - - - - - contractual links; ——————— in-house links.

The lines between television and toy became more closely linked as Mattel and Group W/Filmation enjoyed the privilege of cofinancing. Mattel's sales gained 51% with the success of the television program (Arrington, 1984); Filmation had a successful program subsidized by Mattel; Group W kept the 35% distribution fee in-house (Gelman, 1984). Group W Productions, as a part of the Westinghouse organization, also had viable programming to offer its television stations and cable networks.

THUNDERCATS

In 1985, these arrangements became even more symbiotic with the introduction of *ThunderCats*. this series of characters was developed in a joint meeting between a representative of Telepictures (a syndication company), Rankin–Bass (an animation production company and subsidiary of Telepictures), and Leisure Concepts, Inc. (a licensing agent for the commercial rights to properties and personalities).

Where, with the Smurfs, there were distinct lines between toy production and program production and He-Man had contractual links between Mattel and Filmation, ThunderCats was clearly toy/television:

> [Leisure Concepts] assisted in the initial development of the "ThunderCats" concept . . . [and] acts on behalf of Lorimar–Telepictures Corp. as exclusive worldwide licensing agent for products based on "ThunderCats." . . . "ThunderCats" began in the Fall of 1985 . . . syndicated by Telepictures, a television producer and seller of syndicated TV products. LJN Toys Ltd. is the master toy licensee for "ThunderCats" . . . [with] in excess of 56 domestic and 80 international licenses . . . including party favors, beach towels, toys, games, linen, crayons, juvenile clothing and shoes, lunch pails and thermoses, Halloween masks, dinnerware, sleeping bags, sunglasses, balloons, stickers and books. (Leisure Concepts, 1986b, p. 5)

The links between the production of the toy (developed by a toy licensing agent—LJN Toys),[3] the production of the cartoon, and the distribution of the program, were all now more closely joined.[4] And economic profits were shared; LCI received a percentage of the profits from television syndication revenues, videocassette sales, and licensing fees (Leisure Concepts, 1986b). The licensing activity for ThunderCats generated close to $10 million in gross royalties (1985–1987), and LCI earned what they defined as "significant revenues" from their share of Lorimar/Telepictures profits ("Leisure Concepts Marks," 1987). In addition, Telepictures received 8% of the revenue from toy sales (Sobel, 1985).

As a Toy

The tale of the ThunderCats is, like He-Man, the story of "fantasy, timelessness, and good versus evil."

> From beyond any known galaxy, bringing with them the law and ideals of their doomed planet, ThunDERa, come the THUNDERCATS. JAGA, the wise ... TYGRA, the invisible ... CHEETARA, the quick ... WILYKAT & WILYKIT, the junior cunning duo ... PANTHRO, the deadly ... and SNARF. THE THUNDERCATS—all sworn to serve their young Lord LION-O and to instruct him in the secrets of the "Eye of ThunDERa."
>   Pursuing the THUNDERCATS to Third Earth and determined to possess the "Eye" for their own evil purposes are the hideous MUTANTS from the planet PLUN-DARR, led by the reptilian S-S-SLITHE. They form an unholy alliance with the ageless devil-priest MUMM-RA. (Telepictures, episode 1)[5]

And by raising his sword, Lion-O (good) gains strength and calls the others to battle Mumm-Ra (evil). For "wherever evil exists, Mumm-Ra lives" (Telepictures, episode 2). Each story is a morality play. And each character is sold separately by LJN Toys, Ltd.

Interestingly, LJN Toys, Ltd., the master licensee, owned no production plants but worked on contract with other companies to manufacture toys ideas. From 1980 to 1985, it grew to be one of the top 20 toy producers,[6] and based on its success with the action toys of ThunderCats, LJN Toys reported record revenues in 1985 (Leisure Concepts, 1986b), maintaining that position into the 1990s (Walley, 1995). Although successful, particularly for LJN Toys, the retail sales of the ThunderCats paraphernalia never matched that of He-Man or the Smurfs. However, the idea is to offset production costs and *minimize* risk (Walley, 1995).

As Television

The ThunderCats are important here, not for their success as a toy, but for the innovations they brought to the television marketplace. The first was the arrangements made around the television special that introduced the program. The second was the unique financial arrangements they offered the independent television stations. But the third, their creative genealogy coming from a corporate meeting between the licensing agent and the productions house, was the most significant.

Before release of the program's weekly series, Telepictures offered a longer version as a prime-time movie to television stations with the following three conditions:

1. That the program would be aired once during the early weeks of October.
2. That the program would be offered during children's prime-time viewing hours (6:00–10:00 P.M.).
3. That the program would be run again as a five-part, half-hour series during the November ratings period. ("Lor-Tel Woos," 1986, p. 46)

This innovative introduction created interest for the program, allowed high visibility, and generated production-cost money from the six commercial minutes in the original showing ("Ah, So," 1985). The production costs for the special were recovered through release to the home-video market ("Lor-Tel Woos," 1986).

The second innovative arrangement that Telepictures brought to the television market was profit sharing of the retail merchandise sales. The series costs were invested upfront by Telepictures, but the company needed a strong commitment from television stations. In an increasingly competitive first-run market, profit sharing was designed to give Telepictures an advantage.

> Unlike a major television network or producer, independent producers like Telepictures cannot spread the risk of producing original programming over a vast number of shows. In a case such as *ThunderCats,* where Telepictures' production cost will comprise a substantial segment of total shareholder equity, up-front commitments to share the risk are absolutely necessary to get the program underway. (Federal Communications Commission, 1984, p. 3)

Because of the strong commitment for airtime needed in barter arrangements, Telepictures introduced the concept of profit sharing from merchandise sales.[7] In return for a 3-year commitment, early sign-up stations were offered one of two options: Either the station could obtain a percentage of the net profits from program distribution and from merchandising rights, or the station could elect to receive a higher percentage of the net profits derived from distribution, excluding merchandising rights (Federal Communications Commission, 1984, p. 5).

Profit-sharing, or points, from the distribution of the program was not particularly new; however, the idea that a station could profit from the sales of an advertised product in their market was innovative. The philosophy behind this arrangement was explained by Michael Garin, president of Telepictures:

> Broadcasters who share the risk by signing up early to air the series before there is even a script should also be able to share in the program's profits if it is a success. (Pagano, 1984, p. VI-1)

The program was a ratings success: After the first week on the air, it was the number-one children's program in its time period (children ages 2–11); in the October 1985 NSI/Cassandra's, it was number one in 18 of the top markets (children ages 2–11). By November, Telepictures was claiming, in full-page advertisements, that it was number one in 62 markets.

Internationally, merchandise was licensed in France, England, Brazil, Australia, and Latin America. The program was sold to over 25 foreign markets, including Sri Lanka, South Africa, Taiwan, and Ireland. In fact, during the summer of 1988, one could find the full assortment of ThunderCat action figures in the BBC shop in New Castle-Upon-Tyne, England.

Corporate Structure

Whereas previous arrangements involved clearly defined links between toy, licensing, or production costs (the *Smurfs*), or cofinancing agreements between toy and television companies (He-Man), the investments of ThunderCats were shared between all. Agreements included 8% of toy revenues to Telepictures and a percentage of Telepictures' net profits on syndication revenue, videocassette sales, and program licensing fees to LCI.

These links are demonstrated in the Figure 4.6.

The lines are now more complex as the relationship between licensing agent (Leisure Concepts, Inc.) and production company (Telepictures) demonstrate more direct involvement. Both the licensing agent and the production company were involved in developing the character concept as creativity was moved into the boardroom. The rights to merchandising were given to a "master licensee," and program development was incorporated in-house. Rankin-Bass produced the ani-

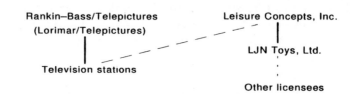

Rankin–Bass/Telepictures   Leisure Concepts, Inc.
(Lorimar/Telepictures)

LJN Toys, Ltd.

Television stations

Other licensees

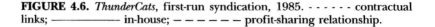

FIGURE 4.6. *ThunderCats*, first-run syndication, 1985. - - - - - - contractual links; ——————— in-house; – – – – – – profit-sharing relationship.

mated series, and distribution and syndication were controlled by their parent company, Telepictures. A new financial configuration was introduced, profit sharing of merchandise, that offering a unique economic arrangement between production and distribution.

Thus, over time, the economic relationships become more complex or more simple, depending on your point of view. From the relationship of Smurfs/the toy and *Smurfs*/the cartoon, to the development of ThunderCats as toy/cartoon the involvement between the toy and television industries is more interdependent. Since the introduction and success of He-Man and ThunderCats, those in the business have come to recognize the importance of this dependency. Ronald McDonald hosts the *Ronald McDonald Family Theater,* and the toy company Tyco introduces its product with a videocassette, because during market testing, young boys proclaim the importance of a television program. According to one sophisticated 8-year-old, television is important to "educate people about the product" (Stern & Schoenhaus, 1990). And meanwhile, Chester Cheetos, a snack-food character, looks for a good script. Although all programs are not developed and produced under these conditions, the importance of considering the child as both audience and consumer is now well established.

The high-risk nature of production, program or product, has encouraged sharing the investment costs to as many agents as possible: Manufacturer, advertiser, licensing agent, syndication company, distribution house, and television stations all become a part of the investment process. This ensures profitability, spreads economic risk, and opens new markets. The toy industry can ensure profitability with guaranteed advertising; production companies spread the high cost of animated programming by bringing in revenue from toy and food companies, and television stations can have first-run programming with minimal investment. By the mid-1980s, this pattern of programming and merchandising and licensing became a standard in commercial broadcasting.

The structure of the children's entertainment business during the late 1980s takes yet another form as competition comes, not only from within the commercial sector but also from alternative media forms such as the growing cable industry. The advertiser-driven model presented here is modified to reflect new configurations as user fees and subscriber support become a part of the marketplace. These changes validate Melody's (1973) prediction that there would be a trend toward specialization in the marketplace as new delivery systems such as Nickelodeon and the Disney Channel present alternatives to the commercial broadcasting system. In the next chapter, the relationships between programming and merchandising in children's cable programming and in public broadcasting, venues for children's entertainment that were not a part of the debate when Melody was writing in the early 1970s, will be explored.

5
◆◆◆

Alternatives

Like most discussions of children's entertainment, the focus here has been on commercial network television. Since the introduction of national broadcasting systems, the networks have dominated children's entertainment. Independent production houses, syndicators, and local stations have contributed to the available entertainment pool, but they work within the commercial system and the standard set by network programming. These next two chapters will consider alternatives for children's entertainment and the ways they have evolved as a consequence of the consumerization of childhood. This chapter will examine the development of cable television and public service broadcasting—alternatives to the dominant commercial networks; the following chapter considers the proliferation of media products such as video- and audiocassettes, books, motion pictures, and computers—alternatives to television.

With the introduction of *Mister Rogers' Neighborhood* and *Sesame Street* on public broadcasting stations in the late 1960s, and the establishment of cable outlets dedicated to children's television in the 1980s, public and cable television have to presented alternatives to the well-established commercial systems.[1] Both introduced the possibility of advertising-free options that Melody (1973, pp. 127–128; Melody & Ehrlich, 1976, p. 125) and others have called for.

The Disney Channel, Nickelodeon, and the Corporation for Public Broadcasting (CPB) present interesting genealogies, such as those explored in previous chapters. These cable services, specifically designed for the child audience, and the public broadcasting system that offers advertising-free children's programming, are significant, for to ignore them would be to ignore an important segment of children's entertainment.

In this chapter the emphasis will be on (1) the role of the Disney Channel as a entertainment dynasty; (2) the development of the Nickelodeon channel as children's own television channel; and (3) the shift in emphasis of public broadcasting from educational/entertainment to entertainment/educational programming.

Since the early 1980s, with new distribution systems such as cable and educational broadcasting, children's television was no longer limited to the offerings of the commercial broadcasters. By the 1983 season, cable supplied almost 70% of children's programming hours; commercial broadcast networks and cable superstations supplied an average of 17% of the hours; and, public stations were responsible for about 10% (Siemicki, Atkin, Greenberg, & Baldwin, 1986; Kerkman, Kunkel, Huston, Wright, & Pinon, 1990). Ten years later, a similar study found that pay or premium and advertiser-supported cable supplied about 68% of the program hours for children, commercial networks and cable superstations supplied about 22% of the programs, and public stations were responsible for about 10% of the children's programs (Pecora, 1993).

In 1973, Melody predicted:

> The nature of market development within the broadcasting industry would indicate that the trend toward specialization in children's programming, as well as other demographically determined, specialized classifications, will not only continue but will also become much more sophisticated. (p. 122)

He continued, "Content diversification and age specificity . . . will be created, but the purpose will be to permit market exploitation. The children's classifications will be based upon the advertisers' interests rather than the child's" (p. 123).

And, indeed, the economic demands of children's programming, have led to a proliferation of age-specific entertainment, not for developmental reasons but to meet economic demands. Action adventure shows with multiple characters are presented to 8- to 10-year-olds, whereas game shows and dramas are programmed to attract tweens and teens: the first tends to advertise toys and accessories; the second, snack foods. All are found on cable.

As illustrated in Figure 4.3, by 1985, advertisers and product manufacturers played a central role in the market structure of the children's broadcasting industry. Returning to Melody's model, similar changes can be demonstrated in cable and public broadcasting.

THE CABLE INDUSTRY

Initially, cablecasting was simply a technology that transmitted television to geographic regions that had difficulties receiving broadcasting signals. Among the first to recognize the potential for cable as a programming service was a New York entrepreneur, Robert Weisberg, who began promoting a cable-distributed Baby-Sitting Network in the late 1960s (Doan, 1969). He programmed cartoons and comedies in the morning for preschoolers and situation comedies for older children in the afterschool hours. Weisberg claimed, "Mother, you see, wants to watch 'Edge of Night' or 'Dark Shadows,' and the kids want to watch 'Felix the Cat' and 'Hercules,' so Mother buys a second line from the cable—for about $1 a month—so they *both* can watch what they want," (cited in Doan, 1969, p. 24). Most of cable television continues to be supported through this system of a user or subscription fee. One would be remiss to disregard Weisberg's other selling point. He claimed that a channel for children would also gain a cable system "Brownie points" with the local chamber of commerce (Doan, 1969).

The Disney Channel and Nickelodeon are two examples of the current profit structure for cable programming services that depend on viewers as audience: The Disney Channel is a premium channel funded primarily by subscriber fees; Nickelodeon is a basic service financed by subscriber fees and advertiser support. Both are systems that program primarily for children. Other programming services such as Showtime, USA, and the Family Channel have some children's entertainment but do not consider children their principal audience.

As is evident through Mr. Weisberg's experiment, children's cable programming is closely aligned with the history of cable programming. The USA Network and HBO first appeared in the New York metropolitan market in 1980; by 1981, USA offered a block of children's programming on Saturday morning and weekday afternoons, and HBO, a premium channel, had occasional programs such as *Peter Rabbit*. Nickelodeon was in place in the New York market by 1982 and offered about 13 hours per day of commercial-free children's programming. The Disney Channel went on-air in the New York market in 1985.

The two cable services under consideration here, the Disney Channel and Nickelodeon, are interesting examples of different cable programming services and a challenge when considering Melody's model. Both appear to offer the alternatives called for by Melody but, in fact, are similar to their commercial competition. One year after it was introduced into the New York market, the Nickelodeon channel was no longer commercial free. Nickelodeon became, according to the then vice-president–general manager, a "major contender for the millions of dollars invested in advertising to reach children" (Forkan, 1984). Although the Disney Channel is "commercial free" it is, by its very nature, one long advertisement for the Walt Disney empire. As fee-driven services, both must meet the needs of individual subscribers (the Disney Channel) or cable carriers (Nickelodeon); they do this within the framework of a commercial system.

When reconstructing Melody's model of market exchange to reflect the relationship of supply and demand, the Disney Channel and Nickelodeon, are represented on both sides of the equation. Not only does the network supply programming and distribution but, to realize a return on its investment through subscriber fees, it also must maintain an audience base, therefore representing the demand side.

The Walt Disney Empire: The Disney Channel

The Disney Channel began programming April 18, 1984. Because of the nature of the Disney empire, the Disney Channel is perceived to be a children's entertainment channel even though 15–30% of the audience, depending on the source, is families without children. Like the Nickelodeon channel, Mr. Weisberg's Baby-Sitting Network, and commercial broadcast stations, programming on the channel follows an age-specific flow with the morning hours for the preschool audience, an afterschool block for older children, and family entertainment in the evening hours. Since its beginning, programming has been a mix of classic Disney and new productions, including a contemporary version of *The Mickey Mouse Club*.

But mostly the Disney Channel is about Disney. Although no products are advertised on the channel, most programs, and its simple presence, reinforce the product name.

As demonstrated in Figure 5.1, this is the ultimate in blurred lines for children's entertainment: Advertiser, licensing agent, program supplier, and market manager are all one.

At present the Walt Disney Company is comprised of three divisions: theme parks and resorts, filmed entertainment, and consumer products.[2] During fiscal year 1992, the consumer products division accounted for over $1 billion in revenue (Walt Disney Annual Report, 1992). This included books, music, computer software, and furniture, all with the Disney imprint. Although the cable channel is not the major source of revenue for the company, its importance for corporate visibility cannot be overestimated. Table 5.1 illustrates the growing importance of filmed entertainment, including the Disney Channel, and product licensing from 1984 to 1992.

The figures in Table 5.1 indicate the volume of revenue generated by the Walt Disney Company during the evolution

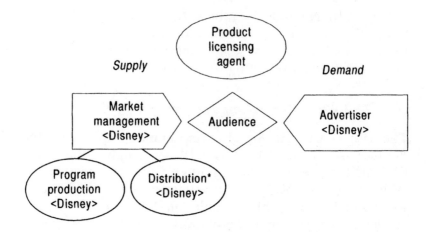

FIGURE 5.1. Market exchange in the Disney Channel, 1990s. *Because of the multiple outlet channels, this is now better described as "distribution" rather than "stations." Adapted from Melody (1973). Copyright 1973 by Yale University Press. Adapted by permission.

of the cable channel. Important to this story is the growth of the children's cable programming and the increase in Disney's television investment in product merchandising, expressed through the incremental growth in proportion of revenue. The Consumer Products division doubled in percentage of revenue (from 7.5% to 14.7%) while Filmed Entertainment, including television and movie production and the Disney Channel, increased by two and a half times it size (from 16.9% to 41.3%). Anyone in the world who has stepped into a retail store or been around children can appreciate the magnitude of these increases.

Disney Merchandising

The Walt Disney Company has been involved in licensing since the earliest days of the company (Grumbine, 1938; Gilbert, 1957; deCordova, 1994). Unlike the ThunderCats and other characters considered merchandising first, the Disney characters generally have been developed as media stars first, although movie releases and toy sales are now simultaneous.

TABLE 5.1. Year-End Revenue (in Millions of Dollars), the Walt Disney Company, 1984, 1988, 1992

	1984 revenue	1988 revenue	1992 revenue
	(% of total revenue)		
Theme parks and resorts	1,098 (75.6)	2,040 (59.4)	3,300 (41.3)
Filmed entertainment	245 (16.9)	1,150 (33.4)	3,100 (14.7)
Consumer products	110 (7.5)	247 (7.2)	1,100 (14.7)
Total revenue	1,453 (99.9%)	3,437 (99.9%)	7,500 (100%)

Note. Totals do not equal 100 due to rounding. Data compiled from Walt Disney Company (1984, 1992); Farhi (1989).

Mickey Mouse was a film star who made the transition to commercial broadcasting and now to cable.

Other characters such as Disney's Winnie-the-Pooh have contributed significantly to corporate revenue. However, the characters most associated with Disney—Mickey and Minnie Mouse, Donald Duck, and Goofy—are "owned" solely by the Disney Corporation, and revenue from licensing is not shared. A recent trend has been to develop age-specific marketing for licensed products using these characters. Among the first of these was the Disney Babies, with over 2,000 products (Walt Disney Company Annual Report, 1992). These baby versions of the Disney stars can be found on products such as disposable diapers and preschool toys. Building on the success of the Disney Babies, Mickey Stuff for Kids and Minnie Mouse products have been developed. Minnie 'n Me is a concept for young girls, developed in 1990 and promoted with media events such as supplements in women's magazines, a music video *The Girls on Minnie's Street,* and an album of *Minnie 'n Me: Just for Girls.*

This is not to say that every program on the Disney Channel offers a line of products, but each mention of Disney or representation of Mickey Mouse or another licensed character is essentially a commercial message.

The Disney Channel Programming

A listing of one weekday's programming on the Disney Channel demonstrates these links between toy and program, as demonstrated in Table 5.2.

A review of the Disney Channel over time demonstrates that this level of original program productions, using Disney characters, is not unusual, and toy and programming tie-ins are not atypical. Generally, the Disney Channel runs from 30% to 50% original programming ("Disney Doings," 1988) with tie-ins for most Disney animated characters. Merchandise

TABLE 5.2. Selected Characteristics of Programming, Disney Channel Daytime Programming, Monday March 14, 1994

	Merchandise tie-in	Production format	Disney-linked production
Care Bears	Yes	Animation	
Disney Presents		Animation	Yes
Dumbo's Circus	Yes	Puppets	Yes
Fraggle Rock		Puppets	
Gummi Bears	Yes	Animation	Yes
Kids Incorporated			
Little Mermaid	Yes	Animation	Yes
Lunch Box		Animation	Yes
Mickey Mouse Club	Yes		Yes
Mousercise	Yes		Yes
Mouse Tracks	Yes	Animation	Yes
Music Box			Yes
My Little Pony Tales	Yes	Animation	
Pooh Corner	Yes	Animation	Yes
Pound Puppies (movie)	Yes	Animation	
Quack Attack	Yes	Animation	Yes
Under Umbrella Tree			
Wonderland			Yes

Note. The New York metropolitan edition of the *TV Guide* is used here as a benchmark for programming. The Disney Channel and Nickelodeon have nationally distributed programming schedules. Data compiled from *TV Guide* (March 12–18, 1994); Disney Channel programming (February 12, 1993); Visit to Toys 'R' Us, Deerfield, Illinois (June 1994).

tie-ins—the availability of toys or other merchandise with the program character's image—exist with over half the programs. Mickey Mouse and other Disney characters are used to promote upcoming programs, and the familiar Mickey Mouse profile is imprinted in the corner of the screen throughout the show—Disney or not. Of the 18 programs identified in Table 5.2, 12 are Disney productions, and 11 have merchandising tie-ins to the characters; seven are Disney productions with product tie-ins.

For the Smurfs, the lines between product merchandising and program production and distribution were distinct, whereas contractual arrangements for the Masters of the Universe and ThunderCats were somewhat more blurred—an idea was developed for both its program and product potential. However, the links between product and production for the Disney Channel are remarkably complex. To sort them out is beyond the scope of this book. One character, Winnie-the-Pooh, originally the hero of a classic storybook, can be found on network television, in afternoon syndication, and on the Disney Channel. He and his friends are found on any retail product that can be sold to children or parents, excluding possibly candy bars, and they are available on records, videotapes, audiotapes, computer games, and story- and picture books. The same is true of other characters such as the Gummi Bears and Chip 'n Dale. With few exceptions, the stable of Disney stars receives exposure in multiple venues—motion pictures, television, audio- and videotapes, computer software, and books—and all are found on licensed merchandise. Each merchandise sale adds to the earnings of the Walt Disney Company through product receipts or licensing fees.

There are numerous examples of Disney characters as media stars, but most of those identified in Figure 5.1 predate the development of product-based characters during the 1980s. One exception is the *Gummi Bears,* the first animated program the Walt Disney Company created for commercial television and product merchandising. Produced in 1985, the show has become a staple on the Disney Channel. Like the other Disney characters, the Gummi Bears can be found in storybooks, records, videotapes, and a wide array of product merchandise. Because they were designed for commercial television and merchandising, they are most appropriate to consider for their contractual arrangements (see Figure 5.2).

Figure 5.2 resembles the distribution of resources for the Smurfs in Figure 4.5; contractual links and corporate relationships are relatively clear. However, it is important to step back and note that here we are talking about not one program, but a system of distribution. Not *A* program negotiated for network or syndicated distribution but rather one part of a whole system called Disney.

As a premium cable channel, the Disney Channel appears to be simply a source of entertainment for its viewers. Yet it is clearly more: It is an entree to *The Wonderful World of Disney*. The Mattel toy company, one of the largest licensees of Disney products,[3] stated in its 1992 *Annual Report* that "the [Disney] characters come to Mattel fully developed, and theater and home video releases and re-releases create unparalleled awareness" (Mattel, 1992, p. 4). Revenue from the sales of Disney products earned Mattel $275 million that year (Mattel, 1992).

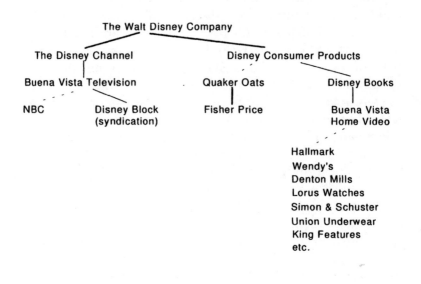

FIGURE 5.2. *Gummi Bears,* 1985–1994. - - - - - - contractual links; _____ corporate relationship.

Nickelodeon

Nickelodeon channel offers another structure of the cable industry and the role commercialism plays in the economics of the children's industry.[4] Whereas the Disney Channel has been supported by subscriber fees and advertising is the corporate image, Disney–Nickelodeon began as a part of cable basic services and, like other commercial systems, depends on advertising revenue. Although other cable networks program heavily for children and are considered family channels, the corporate philosophy of the Nickelodeon channel is that of television for kids (Laybourne, 1993). A day spent watching the channel confirms this.

The channel began as precisely the alternative Melody called for: prosocial, commercial-free programming ("Nickelodeon's Corporate Past," 1989; "Warner–Amex to Charge," 1983). Although it attempts to maintain that programming philosophy, the Nickelodeon channel now carries many of the same commercial messages found on Saturday morning network programming and, in 1993, licensed more than 400 items (Carter, 1994).

Nickelodeon was initially a program called *Pinwheel*, distributed on Warner Cable's experimental QUBE system in 1979. *Pinwheel* evolved into the Nickelodeon channel by 1982; commercial advertising was added in 1983 to supplement user fees, and the channel went to 24 hours of programming in 1985. The majority of children's programs on the Nickelodeon channel are original, live-action productions; programming in the evenings and late at night tends to be reruns of classic, and not so classic, situation comedies; weekends and late afternoons are scheduled with original and perennial cartoons.

To date, the corporate history of Nickelodeon reads like a "who's who" of communication industry giants. The channel was first established by Warner Cable. An alliance between Warner and American Express created Warner–Amex in 1980 and Nickelodeon became a part of Warner–Amex Satellite Entertainment Company (WASEC). With the success of MTV, another WASEC property, WASEC was renamed MTV Networks and the holdings were split three ways between Warner,

American Express, and the public. Five years later, the company was bought by Viacom International. In 1994, Viacom merged with Paramount, making the Nickelodeon channel part of a conglomerate with access to many entertainment venues. (Zitner, 1993; "Viacom–Par Merger," 1994)

Viacom–Paramount
(1994)

Television	*Music*	*Motion pictures*
Cable networks	Radio stations	Studio
Cable systems		Theaters
Television stations		
Syndication rights		

Print	*Entertainment centers*	*Interactive media*
Publishing houses	Theme parks	Software
	Sports teams	companies
	Sports stadiums	

With this merger, the company became the fifth-largest entertainment company in the world, with revenues of $6 billion and an extensive library of television and motion picture programming (Zitner, 1993). Media holdings included networks, production and distribution houses, cable systems, and broadcasting stations. As of 1992, media properties included the following:

> NETWORKS: MTV–Music Television, VH-1, Nickelodeon, Showtime, The Movie Channel, Flix a joint venture with Lifetime channel, Comedy Central, All News Channel
> ENTERTAINMENT: Viacom Productions, Viacom New Media, Viacom World Wide, Ltd., Viacom MGS Services
> CABLE TELEVISION: Systems in California, Oregon, Washington, Wisconsin, Ohio, Tennessee (over 1 million subscribers)
> BROADCASTING: Five television and 13 radio stations. (Viacom, 1992)

Like the Disney Channel, a Consumer Products Group was established in 1992 to supervise character licensing and the development of a merchandising line.

Nickelodeon Merchandising and Advertisements

Unlike the Walt Disney Company, the Nickelodeon channel owned no stable of ready-made characters to license, and few of the Nickelodeon programs lend themselves to merchandising as do the Disney Babies. Nonetheless, in 1994, the *New York Times* reported that the Nickelodeon imprint could be found on 400 items (Carter, 1994) in places like Toys 'R' Us and FAO Schwartz (Triplett, 1994). Among the first of the Nick products was Green Slime shampoo, a perfect beauty aid for the preteen. Green Slime was a trademark of Nickelodeon's *You Can't Do That on Television*. Other products that followed were a home version of the game show *Double Dare,* various clothing items, and paints and craft sets for 6- to 10-year-olds. Nick products are not always program related but often are products that encourage creativity and skill using the Nickelodeon imprimatur.

Nickelodeon productions tend to be live action, competitive game shows, talk shows, dramas, or variety shows that do not lend themselves to merchandising, as do cute animals or animated action heroes. By the early 1990s, the Nickelodeon channel added cartoon programs to the schedule, and the characters from these shows began to find their way to the toy shelves. Mattel and Dakin licensed the rights to a number of productions (Goerne, 1992; Schulman, 1992) and, with the development of an in-house merchandising division, it is clear that the Nickelodeon channel intends to expand the licensing arrangements that have been so successful for others.

The Nickelodeon channel was commercial free during the first 4 years; by 1984, it carried about 8 minutes of local and national advertising. The next year, the company announced its first profit. Prior to introducing commercial advertising, the costs of some programs were partially underwritten by corporations such as Quaker Oats and the M&M/Mars candy company. These underwriting arrangements were similar to the model used in funding public broadcasting programs. The Nickelodeon channel also offered unique sponsorship agreements with several advertisers. For example, Reebok and Converse, producers of athletic shoes, had "exclusivity positions" in the programs *Double Dare* (Reebok) and *Finders Keepers* (Converse) ("Big Advertisers," 1989).

Although the minutes of advertising on Nickelodeon tend to cost less than commercial stations, the environment is still one that encourages consumption. During one hour of *Doug* and *Rugrats,* two of Nickelodeon's most popular programs, 14 different products were advertised promoting cereals, snacks, and fast-food restaurants. All the commercials had also been found on comparable programming distributed by network (ABC) and cable (the Family Channel) stations (Sunday, June 12, 1994, 10:00–11:00 A.M.; Boston, Massachusetts, market).

Nickelodeon Programming

The advertising environment at the Nickelodeon channel, like the programming, increasingly resembles the broadcast networks. A look at the change in programming over 10 years indicates shifts similar to commercial programming: an increase in animation and product tie-in programming. Table 5.3A illustrates that during the early days of Nickelodeon, the channel relied heavily on live-action programs; the few cartoons were imports.

Five years later, the programming on the Nickelodeon channel began to reflect the commercial broadcasting environment, though still relying heavily on live-action. Table 5.3B illustrates both a shift in the type of programming, from live action to animation, and in the number of programs offered (from 12 to 21; not to be confused with the number of hours programmed, because often the shows were run multiple times during the day or for long blocks of time).

Now, in addition to live-action dramas and variety shows (*Lassie, Dennis the Menace, Elephant Show, Fred Penner,* and *Eureeka's Castle*), a number of animated programs both imported (*Little Prince, Adventures of Little Koala, World of David Gnome, Noozles, Inspector Gadget, Count Duckula*) and U.S. (*Heathcliff, Looney Tunes*) were found on the schedule. In-house production increased with *Count Duckula,* a coproduction with Thames Television International of London.

TABLE 5.3A. Nickelodeon Channel, Selected Characteristics of Programming, Monday, October 29, 1984

	Merchandise tie-in	Production format	Production affiliation
Adventures of Black Beauty			
Belle and Sebastian		Animation	
DangerMouse		Animation	
Going Great			
Lassie			
Mr. Wizard			Yes
Nick Rocks			Yes
Pinwheel (5-hour block)			Yes
Third Eye		Not available	Not available
Today's Special			
Who Spooked Rodney		Not available	Not available
You Can't Do That . . .			Yes

Note. Data compiled from programming listings: *TV Guide*, New York metropolitan edition (October 27–November 2, 1984); various resources used to identify production affiliation.

Five years later, and 10 years after program listings for the Nickelodeon channel were available, the programming moved yet closer to the commercial model (see Table 5.3C). The classics remained (*Mr. Wizard, Lassie,* and *Dennis the Menace*), but there were new live-action productions (*What Would You Do*), and off-network cartoons (*Muppet Babies, Alvin, Looney Tunes,* and *Bullwinkle*). Forty-three percent of Nickelodeon's programming was now animation.

Although the change has been gradual, it is evident that there have been shifts in the Nickelodeon channel's programming. In the early days, the shows were primarily live action. As Nickelodeon demonstrated a successful track record with the young audience, advertisers were more willing to invest in commercial time. This provided the channel with the capital to invest in more original and diverse programming but also pushed the channel toward the commercial model set out by Melody. Ten years after taking on advertising, animation and product tie-ins increased. These changes, illustrated in Table 5.4, demonstrate a subtle move toward the commercial structure of programming—heavily animated, half-hour programming, with merchandising tie-ins.

TABLE 5.3B. Nickelodeon Channel, Selected Characteristics of Programming, Monday, October 2, 1989

	Merchandise tie-in	Production format	Production affiliation
Adventures of Little Koala		Animation	
Count Duckula		Animation	Yes
Dennis the Menace			
Don't Just Sit There			
Elephant Show			
Eureeka's Castle	Yes		Yes
Fred Penner's Place			
Heathcliff		Animation	
Inspector Gadget		Animation	
Lassie			
Little Prince		Animation	
Looney Tunes	Yes	Animation	
Make the Grade			Yes
Mr. Wizard's World			Yes
Noozles		Animation	
Pinwheel		Animation	Yes
Super Sloppy Double Dare	Yes		Yes
Think Fast		Not available	`
Today's Special		Not available	
World of David Gnome		Animation	
You Can't Do That . . .			Yes

Note. Data compiled from programming listings: *TV Guide*, New York metropolitan edition (September 30–October 6, 1989); various resources used to identify production affiliation.

Gone were programs such as *Pinwheel*; by 1994 there were more cartoons such as *Alvin and the Chipmunks* and *Dennis the Menace*. Overall, though, the proportion of new and creative programs remained constant. Where Nickelodeon offers an interesting change is in the combination of product and corporate licensing. There has been limited, though increasing, merchandising of the Nickelodeon characters such as *Doug, Rugrats,* and *Ren and Stimpy,* however, it is the Nickelodeon "brand" that is promoted in the FAO Schwartz and Toys 'R' Us stores. Merchandise products carry the Nickelodeon label. Because of Nickelodeon's limited move into the merchandising arena, at this time, it is difficult to develop a corporate genealogy like that for the Smurfs, He-Man, ThunderCats, and Gummi Bears. There have been an increasing

TABLE 5.3C. Nickelodeon Channel, Selected Characteristics of Programming, Monday, March 14, 1994

	Merchandise tie-in	Production format	Production affiliation
The Alvin Show		Animation	
Bullwinkle		Animation	
Cappelli and Company			
David the Gnome		Animation	
Dennis the Menace			
Doug		Animation	Yes
The Elephant Show			
Eureeka's Castle	Yes		
Flipper			
Hey Dude			Yes
Janosch's Dream World		Animation	
Just So Stories		Animation	
Legends of Hidden Temple			Yes
Littl' Bits		Animation	
Looney Tunes	Yes	Animation	
Muppet Babies	Yes	Animation	
Salute Your Shorts			Yes
Weinerville			Yes
What Would You Do?			Yes
Wild and Crazy Kids			Yes

Note. Data compiled from programming listings: *TV Guide*, New York metropolitan edition (March 12–March 18, 1994); various resources used to identify production affiliation.

number of products for Ren and Stimpy, Rugrats, and Doug, but to date they have been limited to plush animals and T-shirts that attract the tweens. Merchandising for these characters has been nowhere near the investment from the Walt

TABLE 5.4. Programming Changes on Nickelodeon, 1984, 1989, and 1994

	1984 ($n = 12$)	1989 ($n = 21$)	1994 ($n = 20$)
Product tie-in	0	3	3
Format			
Animation	2	8	8
Nonanimation	7	11	10
In-house productions	4	8	7

Note. Data compiled from programming listings: *TV Guide*, New York metropolitan edition (October 1984, 1989, 1994).

Disney Company or the ubiquitous nature of the Smurfs in the early 1980s.

However, the Nickelodeon channel, and its parent company Viacom, Inc., offer new possibilities when thinking about corporate genealogies: direct access to the child audience as predicted by Melody, through age-specific programming.

Age-Specific Programming

A major concern of those committed to quality children's programming has been age-specific entertainment, that is, programming designed to meet a child's developmental needs and cognitive abilities. At one level, television does program to an audience based on age with cute cartoons in the early morning hours for the preschooler and action adventure in the later morning or afternoon for the 6- to 10-year-olds. As predicted by Melody (1973, pp. 122–123) "the trend toward specialization . . . [will be] based upon the advertiser's interest rather than the child's." Age-specific here does not consider the developmental or cognitive needs of the child but, rather, commercial pricing and demand and audience availability.

Viacom, through the MTV Network and Nickelodeon, has most institutionalized these commercial principles for children's programming. There are three cable channels under the umbrella of MTV Network: VH-1, MTV, and Nickelodeon. Each of these channels address a particular population. Whereas the networks, and even Disney, attempt to reach a wider audience, these channels have very specific constituents (see Figure 5.3).

In addition to meeting commercial demand with age-specific programming, the Nickelodeon channel also considers children's interests and abilities. In the 1994–1995 season, building around the showcase program *Eureeka's Castle,* the company invested heavily in several new programs for preschoolers (Carter, 1994).

This comes at a time when preschoolers, as a market, are gaining the attention of advertisers. Geraldine Laybourne, then-president of Nickelodeon, explained that "preschool programing was not always an easy sell to advertisers. . . . But

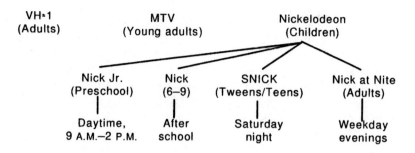

FIGURE 5.3. MTV network structure, 1994.

more and more agencies are recognizing the 'extraordinary' influence that preschoolers can have on their parents" (Brown, 1994, p. 53; Carter, 1994). Certainly, if advertisers are recognizing the potential of a preschool market, can a kiddie channel be far behind? For both merchandising possibilities and advertising dollars, the commercial model identified by Melody can now be applied to the Nickelodeon channel. Like Disney, the Nickelodeon name becomes the corporate product. In many ways, Nickelodeon also carries the ambiance of public broadcasting, with the emphasis on programming that is both entertaining and educational—aside from advertising minutes. However, increasingly, public broadcasting has also become more commercial-like.

PUBLIC BROADCASTING

From its beginning, public broadcasting has had a strong commitment to children. *Sesame Street* and *Mister Rogers' Neighborhood* are held up as the standard for quality children's programming. In addition to these two programs, there have been a number of other shows that demonstrate educational programming can be entertaining. Unfortunately, because of the vagaries of funding, public broadcasting, like Nickelodeon, has begun to take on the characteristics of commercial broadcasting. Although there are no advertisements, there is corporate underwriting, some of which becomes identified with a particular show. For example, in 1991, the Children's Television Workshop (CTW) received a grant from Nike, the maker of sports shoes, for *Ghostwriter,* a weekly series on literacy for 7- to 10-year-olds (Shister, 1991). Although one wants to applaud Nike for its altruism, one must also recognize that Nike is the leading athletic shoe company in the highly competitive youth market. Its logo is shown with each *Ghostwriter* episode, thus associating product and program.

Public television in the United States is the result of a number of events, brought together with the Carnegie Report in the late 1960s. PBS, as a network, was created from a patchwork of stations that had previously broadcast mostly instructional and experimental programming from a variety of educational and public institutions. As an alternative to commercial systems, the intent was that public broadcasting would present the diversity of voices that is the American public. The Carnegie Commission proposed funding be the responsibility of a licensing fee or tax on television sets.[5]

Public broadcasting is organized around three divisions:

1. The *Corporation for Public Broadcasting* (CPB) facilitates training, research, and development, and supports programming through grants and contracts.
2. The *Public Broadcast Service* (PBS) serves as a network between public stations; coordinates program distribution, and provides marketing support.
3. The *local stations* distribute programming and, in some cases, produce programming.

Stations obtain programs from several sources: in-house productions, syndication, and PBS. PBS, in turn, obtains its nationally distributed children's programming from these sources as seen in Table 5.5.

When Congress established the organizational structure for PBS in the late 1960s, a long-term funding base was never authorized. Consequently, as government support declined, stations have turned to nongovernment sources that look suspiciously like audiences (subscribers) and advertisers (foundations and underwriters).

Because it was established to serve the public rather than a marketplace economy, the structure of early public television resists the application of Melody's model, which has been used throughout this book. The intent of public broadcasting was not to meet the "demands" of an economic system or audience but rather was to provide a forum for debate for a public. It was to

> be the visual counterpart of the literary essay, should arouse our dreams, satisfy our hunger for beauty, take us on journeys, enable us to participate in events, present great drama and music, explore the sea and the sky and the woods an the hills. It should be our Lyceum, our Chautauqua, our Minsky's, and our Camelot. It should restate and clarify the social dilemma and the political pickle. (E. B. White, cited in Hoynes, 1994, p. 50)

TABLE 5.5. Program Production Sources, Children's Nationally Distributed Programs, Public Broadcasting, 1990s

Independent producers	
Children's Television Workshop	*Sesame Street*
	Ghostwriter
Family Communications	*Mister Rogers' Neighborhood*
Lancit Media Corporation	*The Puzzle Works*
Lyons Group	*Barney & Friends*
Quality Family Entertainment	*Shining Time Station*

Independent producers/television stations	
Paragon Entertainment/ WTTW, Chicago	*Lamb Chop's Play-Along*
Buena Vista Television/ KCTS, Seattle	*Bill Nye the Science Guy*
Scholastic Productions/So. Carolina ETV	*The Magic School Bus*

Television stations	
KCET, Los Angeles	*Storytime*
WTVS, Detroit	*Club Connect*
WGBH, Boston/ WQED, Pittsburgh	*Carmen Sandiego*
WGBH, Boston	*Long Ago and Far Away*

It was to be a window on the world for our children, but, increasingly, it can also seem like preparation for a trip to the toy store.

Public Television Funding

Initially, public broadcasting challenged the model of market exchange because, as Rowland and Tracey (1993, p. 34) point out: "The argument for public broadcasting in the U.S. remains largely one of its role as an *alternative* to the dominant system" [emphasis in original]. Public broadcasters do not sell audiences to advertisers; however, public broadcasting is nonetheless dependent on its audiences. Audiences are needed to solicit government support, motivate corporate underwriters, and provide local contributors.

Over the past decade, funding sources have shifted from the public support intended by the Carnegie Commission to private funding through corporations and individual subscribers from the community. The percentage of federal to private monies has dropped dramatically. In 1973, public funding accounted for about 70% of the funding to public broadcasting; in 1983, that figure was closer to 50%; and in 1990, funding from public monies declined to 46% (Hoynes, 1994, p. 91). Private sources, including viewers, foundations, and businesses, have increased proportionately (see Hoynes, 1994).

One implication of this increased reliance on private funding has been a greater concern with the composition of the audience. There is a need to consider both the demands of the corporate sponsors and the interests of the audience. This was played out in spring 1994, when upscale automobile companies, financial corporations, and companies such as American Express began investing in public broadcasting; the director of corporate marketing for WNET/New York claimed "PBS's 25 to 35 plus audiences are a highly desirable demographic for automakers" ("Public TV Attracts," 1994, p. 39).

There is no direct evidence that these "underwriting" arrangements do, in fact, influence the final product. Situations such as the early days of radio, where the sponsor sat in a booth and gave thumbs up or thumbs down, do not exist.

However, one can speculate that these arrangements influence the final product in at least two ways: There is a level of self-censorship involved when the writers, directors, and talent work to perceived expectations, and resources are invested in programming that will most likely be "successful" (Goldman, 1985). That success comes to be defined, as in commercial systems, with audience. Demographics becomes the language, and ratings become the currency.

Consequently, the model of supply and demand used to demonstrate the relationship of commercial systems can, after all, be applied to that of public broadcasting.

These changes indicate a shift from the public-service vision of broadcasting, one that views the audience as a democratically constituted public, and its role as an alternative system with a mandate for diversity, to a more commercial vision, with programming that targets a consumer market. Now, we can overlay our model on the process of public broadcasting.

In Figure 5.4 the Market Managers, PBS and the local stations, are a part of both supply and demand creating and distributing programs. *Ghostwriter* fits this model well. The program was created to draw a particular audience to the network, primarily because the preteen audience was not being served by the industry in general, but also because they are, after all, future viewers and a group that influences family viewing patterns. CTW and PBS are the Market Managers involved in production and distribution, and creating the demand for a subscriber base. Underwriting the program is Nike. Subscribers are an audience and a resource as they vote with their dollars and recognition of the Nike brand.

Merchandising and character licensing fees are generally owned by the production house, so, until recently, these fees played only a small part in the model of public broadcasting. Because programming is funded by public money and funds are very limited, this has become problematic for public broadcasting. The argument is made that any revenue from licensing fees should be reinvested in public broadcasting rather than serve as profit.

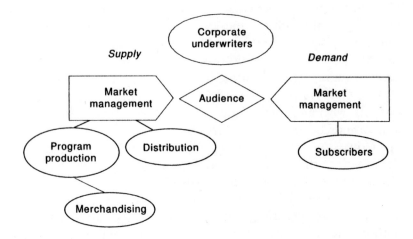

FIGURE 5.4. Market exchange in public broadcasting, national organization, 1990s. Adapted from Melody (1973). Copyright 1973 by Yale University Press. Adapted by permission.

Public Television Programming

The promise of public broadcasting has been commercial-free, quality entertainment. Prior to the Carnegie Report that defined public broadcasting programs were educational courses offered for college credit, frequently repeated educational documentaries, or experimental videos. In the late 1960s, responding to a number of social and economic challenges, public broadcasters began to examine new ways of serving their constituents. The Carnegie Corporation Report concluded:

> Television is not only the child's window on the world, it is also his Pied Piper, sorcerer, and story teller. And television, whether we like it or not, is also the preschooler's unaccredited teacher (The Network Project, 1973, p. 25).

Public television was seen to be a viable alternative to commercial programming, particularly for the underserved, such as preschool children. *Sesame Street* debuted in 1969, joining *Mister Rogers' Neighborhood,* a local production out of WQED/Pittsburgh. *The Electric Company* and *Zoom,* for older children, were on the air by fall 1972. Table 5.6 presents a chronology of children's programs on public broadcasting.

What is most interesting from Table 5.6 is the fact that, except for *Sesame Street,* none of the programs prior to 1990 were tied to merchandising and character licensing; on the other hand, *Barney & Friends, Lamb Chop's Play Along,* and *Shining Time Station,* three programs introduced since 1990,

TABLE 5.6. Introduction of Children's Programming on Public Stations in New York Market: WNET, WNYE, WNYC, 1967–1994

Pre-1970	1980–1984	1990–1994
Mister Rogers' Neighborhood	*3-2-1 Contact*	*Barney & Friends*
Sesame Street	*As We See It*	*Bill Nye the Science Guy*
	Bean Sprout	*Carmen Sandiego*
1970–1974	*Don't Look Now*	*Club Connect*
Big Blue Marble	*Family Classics*	*Ghostwriter*
Electric Company	*High Feather*	*Long Ago*
Villa Allegre	*I Am I Can I Will*	*Lamb Chop's Play-Along*
Zoom	*New Voice*	*The Magic School Bus*
	Newton's Apple	*Puzzle Works*
1975–1979	*Reading Rainbow*	*Shining Time Station*
Carrascolendas	*Righteous Apple*	*Storytime*
Freestyle	*Secret City*	
Infinity Factory	*Sonrisas*	
Music	*Wonderworks*	
Once Upon a Classic	*Voyage of the Mimi*	
Rebop	*Zarabanda*	
Studio See		
Turnabout	**1985–1989**	
Vegetable Soup	*DeGrassi High*	
Watch Your Mouth	*K.I.D.s*	
Owl/TV	*Ramona*	
	Secret City	
	Soap Box	
	Square One	
	Supergran	
	Wildside	

Note. Data compiled from programming listings: *TV Guide,* New York metropolitan edition (October issues).

have been merchandised as toys and clothing—in the case of Barney, quite aggressively.

In early 1994, responding to declining audience numbers and competition from the commercial and cable channels, public television made a renewed commitment to children's programming. A daytime block of programming called "PTV: The Ready to Learn Service," was created, commissioning several new programs. Among the new shows introduced were *The Magic School Bus* and *Bill Nye the Science Guy* for older children.

As explained by Ervin Duggan, president/CEO of PBS:

> Public television has never been quite as strong with the older child Nickelodeon and MTV have been enormously successful in attracting that audience in the commercial media. Now we are involved in an effort to become attractive and arresting to that age group, to be fresh and hip but also high-mind and enlightening. (Zimmerman, 1994, p. 50)

Sesame Street meets MTV.

Public broadcasting has also been seeking alternative financial arrangements. Children's Television Workshop productions, such as *Sesame Street* and *3-2-1 Contact*, were supported by an array of resources, including federal and private grants, and corporate underwriting. During the early years, productions were funded by the Department of Health, Education and Welfare; the Corporation for Public Broadcasting; the Carnegie Corporation; the Ford, and the Markle Foundations; and Xerox, the 3M Company, Quaker Oats, and Johnson Wax. The amount of support from these resources has varied, with merchandising fees increasing in importance. By 1975, licensing income for *Sesame Street* accounted for about $3 million ("CTW Sees Record," 1975); 1984 figures were $14 million on 1,700 licensed products (Brown & Fisher, 1984); and, 1993 figures were $30.76 million in expected revenue on 5,000 licensed products (Zimmerman, 1992). These fees revert back into the company and are not considered profit.

With the introduction of new programming, public broadcasting has been turning to other financial partnerships. Three programs offer interesting examples: *Get Real,* a local production; *Bill Nye the Science Guy,* a commercial venture; and *The Magic School Bus,* an independent production. *Get Real* was a coventure between 19 commercial broadcasters and Wisconsin Public Television (WPT). WPT produced the program and syndicated it to local commercial stations. Commercial distribution allowed WPT an increased market reach and audience share, therefore, access to greater recognition and a larger funding pool. With WPT as producer, the commercial stations that broadcast the program have access to a low-cost, FCC-friendly program (Tobenkin, 1994). *Bill Nye the Science Guy* has been a coproduction arrangement with Buena Vista, the Walt Disney television production company, and KCTS, the public television station in Seattle, Washington. The third example, *The Magic School Bus,* is a coproduction with Scholastic Productions, the production branch of Scholastic Publications, and Nelvana, a commercial animation firm. Stories are based on The Magic School Bus series from Scholastic Publications. Funding for *The Magic School Bus* came from the National Science Foundation, the Department of Energy, and the Carnegie Corporation, with McDonald's fast-food restaurants involved in the promotion of the program.

With each of these programs, public broadcasting found a way to spread the cost of program production in mutually beneficial ways through coproduction arrangements with the commercial sector. *Get Real* and *Bill Nye the Science Guy* are both associated with commercial television, although a product of public broadcasting. And one need not elaborate on the potential for success of a program promoted by McDonald's.

Merchandising

As is evident with Nike and *Ghostwriter,* it is with the issue of character licensing that public broadcasting comes most to resemble commercial children's programming. As noted, the three preschool programs introduced since 1991 all benefit from merchandising. *Barney & Friends, Lamb Chop's Play-Along,* and *Shining Time Station* have been very successful programs in terms of both audience and merchandise sales.

Over 200 Barney products were available, with estimated sales for 1993 at $500 million and an additional $50 million in licensing fees (Edwards, 1994). *Shining Time Station* had about $175 million in sales in 1992 (Darlin, 1993). According to one writer, "The owners of the hugely popular Thomas the Tank Engine [star of *Shining Time Station*] are paid by the government to promote their toys in public" (Darlin, 1993, p. 126). Although this is a rather simplistic assessment of the arrangements, public broadcasting appears to have made only $317,000 in product licensing fees from all shows in 1991 (Jensen, 1994). As successful as they are, neither Barney nor Thomas can match the economic strength of *Sesame Street*'s 5,000 products and $800 million per year in sales (Bedford, 1993).

However, there is a difference between the old-guard, Children's Television Workshop and the more recent production houses: the Lyons Group (Barney), Quality Family Entertainment (Thomas), and Paragon Entertainment (Lamb Chop). The not-for-profit status of CTW falls within the tradition of a public service system.[6] The new groups at PBS, represented by Barney, Thomas, and Lamb Chop, are employed by for-profit corporations. Although there is no question that any children's program created for public broadcasting has a commitment to quality, the need to consider the bottom line and profitability introduces another dimension to the way business is conducted.

According to some reports CPB and PBS funded between 40% and 50% of *Barney* production costs (approximately $4 million of $14.5 million total production costs) over its first three seasons (Bedford, 1993) yet only received fees from Barney tapes and compact disks (Edwards, 1994), missing out on "Barneymania" and a percentage of the estimated $500 million per year in retail sales (Bedford, 1993). This subsidization of programming is noble but shortsighted. In a letter sent to members of Congress during one battle over public broadcast funding, the president of PBS acknowledged that

PBS received limited funds from *Shining Time Station* merchandise sales. His argument was that the production house for *Shining Time Station,* Quality Family Entertainment, received a small portion of its production funds from PBS, $3 million of $15 million production costs by one estimate (Edwards, 1994). This was used to justify the minimal return on retail sales, estimated at $40 million in 1993, PBS received from them (Edwards, 1994).[7]

Lancit Media Corporation, production house for *The Puzzle Works,* is a for-profit corporation like Quality Family Entertainment and the Lyons Group. However, unlike the others that are privately owned, Lancit is a publicly traded corporation. As a production company, Lancit has been associated with PBS since 1983 through *Reading Rainbow,* a program with limited merchandising in the form of books and teaching materials. With more recent agreements, Lancit keeps most merchandising and licensing fees and foreign broadcast rights. Primary financing for the program is from a grant from the Corporation for Public Broadcasting ($4.5 million) and Southern California Edison ($3.5 million); in addition, Lancit and KCET/Los Angeles signed contracts amounting to over $4 million with Sony and Fisher–Price to market merchandise (Croghan, 1994; Foisie, 1993; Jensen, 1994). In return for its investment, CPB will receive 19% of the licensing and merchandising fees (Jensen, 1994).

In another attempt to build on the success of changing economic arrangements, *Reading Rainbow* has been repackaged for foreign distribution. The original programs and the live-action characters will be augmented for the foreign market; puppets will be introduced as hosts "in order to maximize merchandising opportunities for the show and strengthen its appeal" (Foisie, 1993, p. 32).

With a concern for subscriber demographics and an increased reliance on merchandise licensing fees and private funding in the form of corporate underwriting, audience and advertiser become a part of the lexicon of public broadcasting. It begins to resemble the economic model of commercial media. In children's programming, the entrance of private, for-profit corporations, no matter their intentions, also marks a shift to the commercial model. The emphasis on education/entertainment introduced by the CTW and Fred Rogers in the 1960s flips to entertainment/education as Barney, Thomas, and Lamb Chop become the characters of the 1990s. At the announcement of *The Puzzle Works,* Lancit Media Productions was "approached by virtually every major toy and licensing company in the country to discuss *Puzzle Factory* [the program's original title] product licensing" (quoted in Foisie, 1993, p. 32). As in the commercial industry, the separation of product and program becomes more complex.

This chapter began with a discussion of cable and public broadcasting as alternatives to the commercial systems that have dominated the children's entertainment arena. Nickelodeon, the Disney Channel, and PBS all offered the possibility of advertising-free children's entertainment. But, these "alternatives" function within the context of a profit-driven system and, increasingly, they have adapted to that model. Although cable and public broadcasting were set up in opposition to commercial broadcasting, commercial has come to be the defining factor. Initially, the Nickelodeon channel was commercial-free but within a few years turned to advertising for working capital. Public broadcasting has always set the standard for quality children's programming, and continues to do so, but now reflects the product-oriented shows of commercial television; the advertising-free environment of the Disney Channel is in fact one long commercial for Disney. PBS, Nickelodeon, and the Disney Channel become the brand names that readily identify a place for children's entertainment.[8]

Alternative systems appear to be not so alternative after all.

6
♦♦♦

The Media
Marketplace

Not only have the changing relationship between the toy and
television industries and the shifts in alternative systems such
as cable and public broadcasting influenced the material
culture of children but also two other developments are
important to consider: (1) media have multiplied as user-
friendly technology becomes available, and (2) the use of
licensed characters has moved from television into other
forms of entertainment and leisure. It is now common for
characters like the Smurfs, the Power Rangers, and Big Bird
to be available in multiple forms of media, each offering
expanding audience recognition and another product to buy.
In addition, the Disney stars, Looney Tunes characters, the
Flintstones, and the Muppets have come back as baby versions,
increasing the possibilities exponentially. This chapter will
consider the way these changes have influenced the range of
goods available to the child consumer and the expansion of
products competing for the child audience. Shelves bulge with
books, video- and audiocassettes, and computer software: a
proliferation of products as new technology and new characters enter the media market.

As we have seen, the rising cost of production, both program and product, and the high risk of failure encourage industries to come together in mutually beneficial arrangements, but financial risk is also stabilized through multiple media outlets: *The Adventures of the Care Bears* on the Disney Channel is a reminder of the Care Bears coloring book or storybook bringing in the publishing industry, or the music theme bringing in the record industry, or the videocassettes bringing in the movie industry. Because of their links to multiple outlets the Care Bears are no longer a passing fad but a well-established industry. They are still available in toy stores and on the Disney Channel more than 10 years after their introduction.

Until television, few characters had such longevity. Shirley Temple dolls were available in the 1930s and came back again 20 years later, but few one-dimensional or fictional characters experienced stability over time.[1] Raggedy Ann (and sometimes Andy) was a classic rag doll made popular by a storybook and kept in demand by generations of parents and grandparents; Little Orphan Annie has been kept popular by new productions of *Annie*; and, of course, Mickey Mouse offers an exception to every rule. However, none of these characters had the multiplicity of possibilities offered recent characters. Howdy Doody may have made a record, signed a book deal, and had his picture on lunch boxes, but licensing opportunities were few and did not include the unlimited array of toys or the range of media products now available.

A PROLIFERATION OF PRODUCTS

The current media market is very different from that of the 1950s or earlier, when there were four options—network television, books, radio, and movies. Now, television alone brings far more choices. A child looking for entertainment on television often can select from four network stations, several independent broadcast stations, public television and cable, and sometimes HBO and Showtime. This proliferation is bringing about the market segmentation predicted by Melody in 1973:

> The nature of market development within the broadcasting
> industry would indicate that the trend toward specialization
> in children's programming ... will not only continue but
> will also become much more sophisticated. Indeed, this is
> the way the market system is supposed to work. (p. 122)

Secondary networks (Fox, UPN), some cable stations
(Nickelodeon, Lifetime, and USA), and public broadcasting
"specialize" in child- and teen-oriented programming. Com-
patible industries merge or share production costs: HBO
produces video versions of the popular paperback novel *The
Baby-Sitters Club* series for airing on the HBO cable channel
and renting in the video store (dolls sold separately) or Rabbit
Ears productions creates videos that are scheduled on the
Disney Channel, radio, and available as read-along books and
audiocassettes.

Changes in technology also altered the market as new
technologies have made adult media child-friendly. The "My
First ... " products of Sony and Fisher–Price and the easy
accessibility of adult equipment make even preschool children
technology-literate; audiocassettes and CDs are far more du-
rable that the early records. In some households, the VCR is
equipped with a green mark for the play button and a red
mark for the stop button to simplify the adult technology.
Home computers have further opened up the media market
with interactive storybooks, computer games, and educational
software based on familiar characters. With all of these changes,
the media market place is a far different world than it was
when television was introduced in the 1950s or even 1980
when the Smurfs were introduced.

Print Media

Throughout most of this book, media have been defined in
terms of the broadcasting and movie industries, but comic
books, storybooks, trading cards, coloring and sticker books,
and magazines are also an important part of a child's media
environment. Here, too, product expansion and character
licensing are making their mark.[2] National book stores are

developing specialized stores such as Walden Kids from Waldenbooks. Stores such as Learning Smith, affiliated with public broadcasting, and children's educational toy stores such as Zany Brainy seek out print material, increasing that market; the book section in discount stores and Books 'R' Us boutiques within Toys 'R' Us stores demand more product for the shelves; increasingly, children's print material can be found in grocery stores and wherever families shop (Mutter, 1995).

Comic Books

Since their introduction in the 1930s, comic books have traditional been considered "children's" entertainment. Over the years, comic book heroes such as Superman, Batman, and Wonder Woman have crossed into other media to become television or movie stars. More recently, comic book heroes can be found on read-along tapes, Saturday morning cartoons, and video games, and unlike the earlier lone-hero, they are now teams with multiple characters and complex genealogies. There has also been a resurgence of trading cards featuring characters like Marvel's X-Men:[3] Almost 38% of the children included in a 1991 market study of children collected trading cards; 73% of those who collected were boys, and, 69% were between the ages of 6 and 11 (Simmons Market Research Bureau, Inc., 1991). Characters are advertised as good product representatives because of their heroic-like lives—after all, they don't smoke or drink and therefore won't let you down. It is a commentary on the value of licensed characters and modern life heroes.

Superheroes dominate the industry and particularly the comics aimed at the 9- to 11-year-olds market. Led by the Marvel Group, major comic book characters are increasingly negotiating the move to television. After several attempts to break into Saturday morning television, in 1981 and 1986, the X-Men successfully made the crossover in 1992. Although they had been around for a while, they were finally made into a Saturday morning cartoon series for the Fox television network when Margaret Loesch, president and CEO of Marvel

Productions, Ltd., became head of Fox's Children's Network, demonstrating not only crossover of character but of corporate reality.

Magazines

One of the most interesting intersections of expanding market economy and children's entertainment is in the magazine industry. Magazines have the longest history as children's media. By the late 1800s, magazines like *The Youth Companion* were well-established as entertainment and education for children; in 1944, *Seventeen* magazine was published for the teen market; *Mad,* first published in the 1960s, was an extraordinarily successful satire magazine for the young audience. But, like stores in the shopping mall, the youth magazine industry has come to resemble a junior version of the adult market with *Time for Kids* (*Time* magazine), *Sports Illustrated for Kids* (*Sports Illustrated*), *Spy Junior* (*Spy*), *Pop Sci* (*Popular Science*), and *Zillions* (*Consumer Reports*). *Sports Illustrated for Kids* was designed to reach what the publishers saw as the 16 million children, 8 to 13 years old with $5 billion of their own money and $40 billion of parents' money to influence ("*Sports Illustrated* Launches," 1989). Among the advertisers in these magazines are a mix of youth and adult-oriented products: Cheetos food snacks, IBM computers, and Crest toothpaste.

Often, new magazines are character- or product-specific publications. Disney, Children's Television Workshop, Barbie, Crayola, McDonald's and Burger King, and General Foods all have their own publication. *Disney's Adventures* features stories about current movies, toys, and cartoons starring Disney productions and characters. Children's Television Workshop publishes *Sesame Street* featuring the licensed characters of *Sesame Street. Barbie,* the magazine, is marketed to the young fans of Barbie dolls and features new items and accouterments for Barbie and her friends. *Crayola Kids* is, of course, filled with crafts and things to do with crayons and scissors. *What's Hot,* published by General Foods Corporation contains "advertorials" and recipes for General Foods products among its stories and games—the ultimate in marketing strategies to consumer and audience. These "fanzines" are nothing more than product promotions for the characters.

Books

The children's publishing industry has also grown over the past two decades, indicated by the success of bookstores like Walden Kids. Children's sales have increased considerably in the national bookstore chains (Burroughs, 1989), but as noted earlier, children's media sales are not limited to bookstores. Overall, children's book sales, as a percent of the total leisure book sales, began to increase steadily in the mid-1980s. During the early 1970s, children's book sales were about 15% of the total sales for entertainment books. There was a marked decline during the late 1970s and early 1980s, but by 1985, children's book sales become a more significant part of the market.

It is predicted that children's book sales will continue to increase even though there is a projected decline in the birth-rate (Berry, 1993). Questions of causality are always difficult to prove, but this growth in the children's market, in relation to the adult market, coincides with the surge of character-licensing and other changes in the children's market. In addition, the sales of paperback books have increased from 2% of juvenile book sales in 1971 to over 27% of sales in 1991 and has continued to grow. Changes in the book industry during the 1980s serve well to illustrate the shifts in market and market segmentation that contributed to the growth of paperbacks. An interesting illustration is offered by Simon and Schuster's strategy to reposition the *Nancy Drew Mystery Series*, both segmenting the market and increasing market potential.

Nancy Drew mystery books for young girls, first introduced in the 1930s, enjoyed some media crossover—a Nancy Drew movie in the 1930s and her own television series in 1977, and some merchandising—a Nancy Drew cookbook, for example. But for the most part, the books were a popular mystery series, with new hardback books released once a year from 1932 to the early 1980s. Then, Simon and Schuster acquired the publication rights from a smaller publishing company. Within a year, they were publishing a second line that incorporated elements of the previously successful mystery novels and the growing genre of teen romances. The original story line (the mystery series, *Nancy Drew Series*, ages 11–12) continued to be published, but now there was a new product built on the product recognition of the old (the romance series, *Nancy Drew Files*, ages 12–14). More recently Simon and Schuster has introduced several new variations on students at Nancy Drew's hometown high school (*River Heights* for ages 9–11) and a series that sends her off to college (*Nancy Drew on Campus*). Where once there was one market to sell, there are now four—Series, Files, River Heights, Cases—all building on the reputation and recognition of the traditional Nancy Drew books. In addition, the new series books are paperbacks released monthly, so where there was one product/book per year, there are now over 40 books per year.

This same approach has been used by Bantam Books with their teen series, *Sweet Valley High*; a second series, *Sweet Valley Kids*, was developed for a younger audience of 8- to 10-year-olds; and *Sweet Valley University*. In 1994, stories based on the Sweet Valley High characters were available for television syndication. Further developing this strategy, Scholastic, Inc. brought out several variations of The Baby-Sitters Club: the traditional series, the *Baby-Sitter Little Sister* series, special collections and editions, with stories built around each character in the BSC (Baby-Sitter Club code), and, like Nancy Drew, the Baby-Sitters Club mysteries. A television series and motion picture, produced by Scholastic Productions, Inc., and dolls by Kenner Toys are also available.

New genres as well as new series are introduced too. Building on the popularity of horror films and Stephen King novels, *Scholastic* magazine came out with a series of books by R. L. Stine. This series, *Goosebumps*, is extraordinarily popular and offers the requisite licensed products. According to one source, 160 million books are in print, there are over 44 licenses, and it is a number-one ranked television show (Dugan, 1996).

Like the television industry, the print media now offer multiple products and personalities to a variety of audiences.

Recording Industry

Teens have been central to the music industry since the 1950s and the advent of Rock and Roll, but the younger market has been ignored both in terms of product and technology. One argument has been that the children's record industry does not require the quality sound[4] or costly musicians of the adult market, so juvenile records can cost less than one-tenth of those produced for adults (Newcomb, 1990). The revenue generated is, therefore, inconsequential to the major players in the industry.

Although numbers are not readily available, it is claimed that the children's audience accounts for less than 2% of the market share (Jeffrey, 1993) and, of that market, Disney dominates the field.[5] The size of the children's market is difficult to establish because children's products are underrepresented in record stores, where ranking and market shares are determined by sales. Children's audio products, like books, are distributed in a number of venues: educational catalogs, toy and discount stores, grocery stores, drugstores, and even the children's furniture department, alongside cribs and beds. This makes marketing and promoting time-consuming and inefficient for major companies organized for mass distribution.

However, although marginal, recorded music, record players, and radios have long been a part of children's entertainment, with even the earliest records featuring media characters such as Howdy Doody and Roy Rogers. Peter Pan Records was formed in 1932, and Disney was promoting children's records by the late 1950s. The 1940 Sears Christmas Catalog pictured a "new electric phonograph and carrying case" for children, and by 1950, RCA Victor was advertising a series of children's records featuring the Roy Rogers Rodeo (to be played on a Roy Rogers Victrola phonograph). Using a juvenile version of their mascot, Little Nipper, to define the children's series, RCA promoted the Roy Rogers 45 rpm record of "real rodeo sounds and action," including color pictures and a storybook. Other stars featured in a 1950

Parents Magazine advertisement included Howdy Doody and Disney's Cinderella.

Sales were revitalized in the 1980s when Parker Bros., a toy company, released records based on the then-popular licensed characters, the Cabbage Patch dolls. The Hasbro toy company followed with storybooks and audiocassettes featuring licensed characters: My Little Pony, G.I. Joe, Charmkins, Barbie, and Masters of the Universe ("Parker Bros. Bows," 1984; "Kid's Records Spinning Off," 1984). The strongest move into the children's audiorecording industry came in the early 1990s, when many of the dominant record companies created children's divisions. At least four of the six major record companies—BMG, MCA, Sony, and Time–Warner— started children's labels. In 1996, Rhino Records joined with DIC Entertainment to market records from DIC program characters (Jolson-Colburn, 1996, p. 4).

Renewed interest in children's music was the result of several factors, some similar to those identified earlier with other media: the growing number of children and the rise in toy and gift purchases, the more "cost-effective" price of cassettes compared to many toys, and parents who grew up with music (Zimmerman, 1992).[6] Also contributing to this new status were adult musicians, often themselves parents, interested in the genre (Hinckley, 1991; O'Connor, 1993). Material has become more creative and diversified as reggae and rap join alphabet songs and Mother Goose rhymes. One product that built on several of these factors was albums of lullabies based on instrumental versions of the Beatles music. Produced by a record company founded by a parent, the albums were entitled *Baby Road* (as in *Abbey Road*) and *The White Album* (as in *The White Album*). Each cover built on the images of the adult albums: *Baby Road* had toddlers at a zebra-crossing just like the Beatles in the original album; *The White Album* was a diaper ("Indie Specialists," 1991, p. C12).

Media attention can be one indicator of the current interest in children's music. *Billboard* magazine, the voice of the industry, has had yearly reviews of children's music, but in 1992, recognizing the growth of the children's sector, they added a column, "Child's Play," to cover the topic on a weekly basis (McCormick, 1992a, 1992b).

Because children's music is not supported by radio play, and is market driven, links with successful television programs such as *Kidsongs*; *Sharon, Lois, and Bram*; and *The Elephant Show*, and movies such as *The Lion King* and *Pocahontas*, and preestablished licensed characters are important to sales. The move into the industry by the major record companies has been, in part, because of the availability of readily identifiable personalities. Big Bird and Alvin and the Chipmunks (Sony), Minnie and Mickey Mouse (Disney Records), The Muppets (Jim Henson Records/BMG Kidz), and the Mighty Morphin Power Rangers (Saban/Time–Warner) are just a few of the links between the majors and licensed characters.

Until the 1980s and the success of Raffi, a children's entertainer with a national audience, the children's record industry depended on storytellers and singer/songwriters from independent producers and distributors such as Peter Pan, Round River Records, Shadow Play, or Discovery (now with BMG Kidz). Recognizing the attention to Raffi and this new market of children, major companies began entering the field. Initially, the companies signed creative artists, but the difficulty of promoting their albums (or cassettes or CDs) to children soon became evident (McCormick, 1993a, 1993b, 1994a, 1994b). Young children simply do not shop the record stores for the latest Pearl Jam or Garth Brooks album. Without radio play, or the reputation of a Raffi, sales depend on name recognition. When buying a gift, grandma all to often reaches for a Barney not a Bill Harley.

The children's music industry has undergone a renaissance of sorts. Record sales are up and there are a growing number of child-oriented radio stations and syndicated radio programs offering an outlet for the new songs and stories. Records, cassettes, and CDs can be found next to books and toys, and record stores are increasing shelf space and creating environments for children to browse.

Read-along books and records have also been available since the 1950s, but with easier technology and the proliferation of products based on established characters, the music has become huckster for movies and merchandise to the 3-year-old.

To play the music, corporations such as Sony and Fisher–Price have produced technology with easy-to-push buttons requiring minimal skills. Sony's line of "My First. . . . " 's, such as "My First Boom Box" and "My First Walkman" and Fisher–Price tape recorders, make music accessible and children independent. For Sony, these products served to establish brand-name recognition in the music field to a young audience of potential consumers.

Motion Picture Industry

The movie industry is another particularly volatile business with investment costs committed before the product is made and success dependent on a number of difficult-to-predict factors. Consequently, the industry works to assure profitability by relying on previously successful story lines and the most available audience. For example, after World War II, the industry turned to youth movies to attract the same teen audience that advertising marketers were targeting. Young stars such as James Dean and Natalie Wood assured box office success. More recently, the movie industry has again brought a series of new movies for the youth market. In fact, the movie industry is increasingly fragmenting this audience, with animated movies about the Care Bears for preschoolers, movies such as *Home Alone* and *Home Alone 2: Lost in New York* for the tweens, and almost everything else for the teenager.

The licensing of movie characters has become a business as successful as those connected with television: Witness the marketing of Disney's *The Little Mermaid, Beauty and the Beast, The Lion King, Pocahontas,* and *The Hunchback of Notre Dame. Home Alone 2: Lost in New York* generated over 50 licensed merchandise products, bringing an anticipated $400–$500 million additional revenue beyond the ticket sales. As detailed by one production company's president of Licensing and Merchandising: "What we're trying to do is really capture the fun of the film in a wide range of products for kids" (Rosenfeld, 1992, p. A6).

This market allows a production house another venue from which to recover costs. Character licensing offers up-front investment money not previously available. Movies pre-*Star Wars* rarely offered merchandising agreements, but now such agreements are integral to the financing of a movie. This merchandising is not limited to the child audience: The Batman series marketed products like pajamas, T-shirts, bedding, socks, backpacks, beach towel, boxer shorts, caps, watches, cosmetics, videocassettes, and, of course, cereal to all ages. Nor is the concept limited to people: Characters from *All Dogs Go to Heaven,* a full-length animated movie, were used to sell dog food.

Licensing, product tie-ins, and promotional deals expanded after the success of *Star Wars* in the late 1970s; such economic relationships were rare before then, as movies were seen as having too short a "shelf life" to make such arrangements profitable (Forkan, 1982). With the advent of sequels and the success of the action toys released in connection with *Star Wars,* Hollywood studios and toy companies saw the potential for mutually profitable arrangements. More than 30 companies invested in Columbia Pictures' *Annie,* based on the story of Little Orphan Annie, and Kenner Toy Company released a series of action-adventure toys with each sequel to *Star Wars* (Forkan, 1982).

The success of the Smurfs' motion picture in 1982, the number-one rated Saturday morning cartoon at the time, and *The Adventures of the Care Bears,* based on an established toy and product licensee, also brought recognition to the pre-school market, a segment previously ignored by the movie industry (Greenberg, 1985). Although Disney has made family movies with broad-based appeal, anyone familiar with the Care Bears can see its attraction is primarily to a preschool audience.

Building on this growing market of young movie audiences, a number of production companies affiliated with television and family viewing have become involved in the movie industry: Scholastic Productions with Columbia Pictures and Paramount Pictures, the Discovery Channel with

Sony, and Nickelodeon with 20th Century Fox and Paramount Pictures (Cox, 1995; Dempsey, 1995).

Movie producers, like those in the television industry, have found that a production's shelf life increased through the interest generated by merchandise and the succession of new audience-generations every 3 years. In the early 1990s, a succession of new animated movies were in development that built on children's interest in animation, well-established stories, and merchandising potential. Table 6.1 lists the animated motion pictures in production during the 1990–1992 seasons. All 20 movies were based on well-established stories, previously successful characters, or sequels.

Several of the movies were adult oriented (*Rock-a-Doodle* and *Rover Dangerfield*), but the others were a part of marketing to a family audience. *An American Tail 2* was a sequel to the popular children's movie *An American Tail*; *Oh the Places You'll Go* was based on characters from the well-known Dr. Suess books; and, *Aladdin, Beauty and the Beast, Sinbad,* and *Thumbe-*

TABLE 6.1. Feature-Length Animated Motion Pictures, 1990–1992

Title	Production house
Aladdin	Disney
An American Tail 2	Amblin/Universal Studios
Beauty and the Beast	Disney
Bebe's Kids	Paramount/Hyperion
FernGully: The Last Rainforest	20th Century Fox
The Gumby Movie	Permavision/Mars
Nightmare Before Christmas	Disney
Oh the Places You'll Go	Lightmotive/Tri-Star
Once Upon a Forest	Hanna–Barbera
The Pebble and the Penguin	MGM
Rock-a-Doodle	Sullivan Bluth Studios
Rover Dangerfield	Warner Bros.
Sinbad	Franck Entertainment
The Thief and the Cobbler	Warner Bros.
Tom and Jerry: The Movie	Film Roman/Turner
Thumbelina	MGM/Sullivan Bluth Studios
A Troll in Central Park	Sullivan Bluth Studios
We're Back	Amblin

Note. Data compiled from Ginsberg (1991); Stevenson (1992).

lina were well-established stories; Tom and Jerry and Gumby were familiar to anyone growing up with American television. Not all of these movies gained fame and fortune or box-office numbers, but the point is that all were based on previously successful media characters and all are were produced with "lucrative visions of stuffed toys, theme park attractions and video sell-through" (Brodie & Greene, 1994, p. 55). And all did end up in the videocassette market.

The Disney's animated movies The Lion King, Pocahontas, and The Hunchback of Notre Dame offer interesting examples of prerelease publicity built on merchandising. Because children learn about movies from television, for weeks before release the movies were heavily advertised on television with tie-ins to fast-food restaurants. The Disney Channel frequently ran The Making of The Hunchback of Notre Dame in the weeks before its release. Books and toys were on the shelf before the movies opened, and a trailer for The Lion King was included in the eight million video cassettes of Jafar's Revenge, a direct-to-video sequel to Disney's Aladdin. Those who saw The Lion King in movie theaters saw an 8-minute preview of Pocahontas. Once the movies were released, there was a ready audience.

After going to see The Lion King with a grown-up, a child as young as 3 is primed to pop a tape of the award-winning theme song Circle of Life performed by adult-musician Elton John into the Fisher–Price cassette player and follow along with the Adventures of Simba storybook (while wearing Lion King pajamas and hugging a Lion King doll). That child is also an audience for the videocassette.

Home-Video Market

When The Lion King was released to the home-video market, it sold over 20 million copies in the first day (many stores were taking reservations for copies in the weeks before release), with expected sales to reach 26 million, probably becoming the bestselling homevideo (Sandler, 1995).

No industry has become more closely identified with children's entertainment than the home-video market. Video players/recorders are in almost as many homes as televisions.

A 1990 study of the children's market found that over 80% of the children surveyed lived in households with VCRs; in homes with higher incomes, over 90% of the homes had video players/recorders. Children use the VCR twice the number of hours as adults ("Home VCR Study," 1988).

Video recorders entered the home entertainment market in 1975 with the introduction of Sony Betamax, and from the beginning, children were identified as an important market segment. In 1983, *Variety* reported that there were 20 million potential video consumers ages 3 to 8 years old ("Moppet Aud Is Latest Target," 1983). Children are a unique market for the industry, because unlike adults, children are content to view a cassette multiple times—seldom tiring of a favorite story. Adults tend to buy, not rent, children's videos. In addition, like other media, there is that new generation every 3 or so years as older children lose interest and younger children are ready to replace them. Also, as with the record industry, the production of children's videocassettes tends to be more cost-effective. Many children's videos are repackaged material such as television programs or movies.

Among the first children's videocassettes was *Strawberry Shortcake* in 1982. By 1985, many of the major production and distribution companies were involved in children's videos. Table 6.2 demonstrates some of the connections between early home-video distributors and production companies.

Most interesting in Table 6.2 is the expansion of markets demonstrated by the move of publishing houses and toy companies into the video production arena. Western Publishing, home of Little Golden Books, is involved in the video market as well as publishing books and producing records. Random House, one of the major publishing houses, also distributes Children's Television Workshop videos. DC Comics and Marvel Comics and Hallmark Properties of Hallmark greeting cards are also producers.

Again, the links between toy and entertainment are strong. As reported in one industry story:

> The backing of toy companies is becoming critical to the success of children's video, and, since toy manufacturers

TABLE 6.2. Production and Distribution Companies, Home-Video Market, 1985

Distributors	Production companies	Characters
Kideo Video	LBS Communications DIC Enterprises	*MASK* *Gobots* *The Adventures of the Care Bears*
Prism Entertainment	Marvel Comics Video	*Spiderman* *Fantastic Four* *Incredible Hulk* *Spiderwoman* *Captain America* *Mighty Thor*
Random House Home Video	Children's Television Workshop	*Sesame Street*
Walt Disney Home Video	Hasbro Bradley	*Wuzzles*
RCA/Columbia Pictures Home Video	Group W/Filmation/ Mattel	*Princess of Power*
Vestron Video	Hallmark Properties Kenner	*Hugga Bunch* *Robotman*
Warner Home Video	DC Comics	*Super Friends*
Western Publishing	Western Publishing	*Little Golden Books*

Note. Data compiled from Harmetz (1985); "Kideo Video" (1985); "Prism's Marvel Library" (1985); Melanson (1985a, 1985b).

are able to spend many times more promo dollars than a video company could ever consider, cross-promotional linkups with the toy business can give children's vids a significant boost. ("KidVid Forces," 1987, p. 47)

During one year (September 1984–September 1985), children's video sales were dominated by Disney and toy-based programming. Table 6.3 documents the top children's titles from sales and their production source.

Fourteen of the cassettes were Disney products, of the seven non-Disney videos, all were recycled television programs or movies: *Rainbow Brite* and *Rainbow Brite/Peril in the Pits*; *Transformers/More Than Meets the Eye* and *Transformers/The Ultimate Doom*; *Care Bears Battle the Freeze Machine* and *The Care*

TABLE 6.3. Top Children's Video Sales, Production House and Story Origin, September 29, 1984–September 28, 1985

Title	Production house	Origin
Pinocchio	Walt Disney Home Video	Movie
Life with Mickey	Walt Disney Home Video	Movie
Limited Gold Edition Cartoon Classics: Mickey	Walt Disney Home Video	Movie
Limited Gold Edition Cartoon Classics: Donald	Walt Disney Home Video	Movie
Robin Hood	Walt Disney Home Video	Movie
Limited Gold Edition Cartoon Classics: Minnie	Limited Gold Edition	Movie
Rainbow Brite: Peril in the Pits	Vestron	TV/toy
An Officer and a Duck	Walt Disney Home Video	Movie
Limited Gold Edition Cartoon Classics: Pluto	Walt Disney Home Video	Movie
Donald's Bee Pictures	Walt Disney Home Video	Movie
Transformers: More than Meets the Eye	Family Home Entertainment	TV/toy
Transformers: The Ultimate Doom	Vestron	TV/toy
The Care Bears Battle the Freeze Machine	Vestron	Movie
Limited Gold Edition Cartoon Classics: Daisy	Walt Disney Home Video	Movie
Disney's Best: The Fabulous Fifties	Walt Disney Home Video	Movie
Rainbow Brite & The Mighty Monstomurk Menace	Vestron	TV/toy
The Disney Dream Factory: (1933–1938)	Walt Disney Home Video	Movie
The Care Bears Movie	Vestron	TV/toy
Voltron–Castle of Lion	Sony Video Software	TV/toy

Note: From "KidVideo Chart Review," (October 5, 1985 p. CE-10). Copyright 1985 by BPI Communications, Inc. Reprinted by permission.

Bears Movie; and *Voltron/Castle of Lion* ("KidVideo Chart Review," 1985). Table 6.4 illustrates the continuing trend to recycle television programs. In Table 6.2 *Hugga Bunch* and the series of Little Golden Books, were the only characters not previously television stars.

By 1993, there appeared to be fewer television links to the videos sold, though Disney still maintained market domination and many of the animated movies listed in Table 6.1 were now in distribution for the home market (see Table 6.4).

TABLE 6.4. Top Children's Video Sales, 1992

Title	Distributor	Origin
Fantasia	Walt Disney Home Video	Movie
The Jungle Book	Walt Disney Home Video	Movie
The Rescuers Down Under	Walt Disney Home Video	Movie
101 Dalmatians	Walt Disney Home Video	Movie
Fievel Goes West	MCA/Universal Home Video	Movie
An American Tail	MCA/Universal Home Video	Movie
Peter Pan	Walt Disney Home Video	Movie
Dumbo	Walt Disney Home Video	Movie
Charlotte's Web	Paramount Home Video	Storybook
Alice in Wonderland	Walt Disney Home Video	Storybook
The Little Mermaid	Walt Disney Home Video	Movie
The Land Before Time	MCA/Universal Home Video	Movie
Bambi	Walt Disney Home Video	Movie
Tiny Toon Adventures	Warner Home Video	TV/toy
The Great Mouse Detective	Walt Disney Home Video	Movie
All Dog's Go to Heaven	MGM/UA Home Video	Movie
Disney's SingAlong Songs	Walt Disney Home Video	TV
The Brave Little Toaster	Walt Disney Home Video	Book
FernGully	FoxVideo	Movie
Sebastian's Caribbean Jamboree	Walt Disney Home Video	Movie/TV
Workout with Barbie	Buena Vista Home Video	Toy
Rock-A-Doodle	HBO Video	Movie
The Rescuers	Walt Disney Home Video	Movie
Ducktales, The Movie	Walt Disney Home Video	Movie/TV

Note: From "Top Kid Videos" (1993). Copyright 1993, BPI Communications, Inc. Reprinted by permission.

Since the children's home-video market was established in the early 1980s, there have been only minor variations in the structure of the market. Although Disney and movies dominate recent sales charts, cross-promotions with restaurants and television and product tie-ins remain important. With success, the producers and distributors of home videos, like the television and the book publishing industry, have looked to new arenas for growth.

Although videos have always met the needs of a wide range of ages, home videos are now heavily marketed to the preschooler as audience segmentation becomes more clearly defined. By 1995, Disney had a preschool series, Bright Beginnings; Jim Henson's Preschool Collection featured the

Muppet Babies; Sony Wonder distributed the preschool programs of Nick Jr. and PBS; and Warner Home Video's KidVision marketed Baby Goes . . . videos (McCormick, 1995).

Sony continues its move into the young market with more than 100 Sony Wonder video titles based on preestablished characters and stories. Titles range from *Tales from the Crypt* (ABC Television) and *Are You Afraid of the Dark* (Nickelodeon) for the tweens to a My First . . . series for preschoolers. In an interesting move away from licensed arrangements, now that Sony Wonder has been established, its next move appears to be into original programming. As explained by the senior vice-president for creative affairs: "One isn't beholden to anyone else. . . . It's good to own the pieces" (Nichols, 1995).

Other Entertainment

Two forms of entertainment rarely included in discussions about the media or the business of children's entertainment that build on the phenomenon of character-based products are games and live concerts. Board games with tie-ins to popular media characters are not new. *Dick Tracy* and the *G-Men,* two popular radio programs, were advertised in the 1936 Sears Catalog. In 1949, Elsie the Cow, the representative for Borden's Dairy Company, had her own game but most games were generic like "Monopoly" or "Chutes and Ladders." After 1980, virtually every licensed character had its name on a board game, and over 80% of the children in Simmons Market Survey owned one (Simmons Market Research Bureau, Inc., 1991). Live concerts and personal appearances were performed by radio personality Bobby Benson and movie star Shirley Temple. In 1990, concerts range from the simple stage presence of the folksinger Raffi to extravaganzas produced by the Power Rangers or the Smurfs on Ice.

Games

Videogames enter the market about the time licensed characters become important. One interesting example of media/game crossover comes from Nintendo, a leader in the industry, and the Super Mario Bros. characters. Nintendo introduced the characters and the Brothers soon were found on Saturday morning cartoons, licensed merchandise, and featured in a popular tween movie *The Wizard* (Kinder, 1991). Writing about the power of media to shape potential consumers, Kinder pointed out that the young star of *The Wizard* comments on the game, "Super Mario Bros. 3," featured in the movie (but not yet on the market): "I never played anything like it before, I can't wait until it comes out and I can buy it!" (p. 95). A remarkable union of media and marketing.

As with other media and toy industries, the game industry builds on character recognition. Although the audience for video games is predominantly young boys and stories are often framed by mythology or "the chase," less malevolent adventures can be found based on the Smurfs or Super Mario Bros. In the 1980s, popular games—"PacMan," "Rubik The Amazing Cube," and "Dungeons and Dragons"—made the crossover to television. From 1982 to 1990, 10 children's cartoons were based on characters that had been games first (Pecora, 1991). Conversely, popular characters have made the crossover, offering new products and character identification to the game industry. With the advancement of technology that made computer games portable and affordable, many characters are available on hand-held computers including Aladdin, the Teenage Mutant Ninja Turtles, and Snow White.

Concerts

Both the Smurfs and Super Mario Bros. were Saturday morning cartoon characters and came to "live" as performers in concert and at the Ice Capades. Following in the tradition of concert appearances by adult stars and early entertainers, a number of the licensed characters have toured the country doing live concerts promoting retail sales and media events. Alvin and the Chipmunks, the Muppet Babies, the Teenage Mutant Ninja Turtles, Barney, and the Mighty Morphin Power Rangers have performed in concert. Mattel's He-Man and the Masters of the Universe and Barbie appeared in live shows, and the Care Bears, Strawberry Shortcake, and all characters worth a costume, have appeared at openings and in shopping malls.

One of the few people-characters who started out in the live concert venue and have been successful as licensed characters are the New Kids on the Block. A rock group with a strong tween following, they had their own Saturday morning cartoon show, number-one album sales, $80 million in merchandising, a clothing boutique in J. C. Penney stores, and a 900 telephone line for their Talking Fan Club (Newcomb, 1990). For several years, the group grossed one of the highest incomes in the industry based on their sales of records and licensed products, concert performances, and other by-products of their fame.

The proliferation of media products has come about during the 1980s through the increasing number of products identified as "children's." A children's movie begets a children's television program, begets a children's album, begets a children's videocassette series, begets a children's storybook, begets an activity book, and a video game. Among the best examples of this phenomenon are two recent animated motion pictures released by the Disney studios: *The Little Mermaid* and *The Lion King*. Both of these films have generated secondary media products, and the Little Mermaid and Timon characters from the movies debuted on Saturday morning cartoons. Not only does character licensing influence sales in product merchandising but it also serves the same purpose in media sales. A Little Mermaid record offers a known quality, the story is familiar, and the quality, generally, is assured.

This increase is the consequence of many of the same circumstances that contributed to the growth of the toy industry discussed in Chapter 3. Social changes led to greater demand for consumer goods and economic stabilization was encouraged with year-round sales and product longevity.

Associated with the growth in media products has been the proliferation of manufactured goods and services. A child of 1, wearing Mickey Mouse diapers, may not be ready to demand a Mickey Mouse storybook—but the time will come— foods, restaurants, diapers, clothes, whatever now build on the exposure offered by the television or motion pictures and the reinforcement of other media. Parents raised on the images of Mickey Mouse and Strawberry Shortcake buy the familiar images for their children ("Mickey and Bambi," 1992). When competition is intense and stability an objective, tie-ins assure an edge—plain diapers or cute little Disney diapers, a storybook about a talking mouse, or a storybook about Mickey Mouse.

Now, in addition to a television show, the media-wise child can have the same program on videocassette, in paperback, on audiotape, and probably as a video game. In some cases, this proliferation is the result of a new technology or a technology that was not previously child-friendly. VCRs and boom boxes for the preschool set were simply not available 10 to 15 years ago for the child or adult. Other changes are the result of an increase in possibilities. Children are now considered an appropriate market for computer games, and audio- and videotapes. An informal survey of Disney's new motion picture release *The Lion King* reveals crossover media representation in books, comic books, coloring and activity books, trading cards, audiocassettes, CDs, MTV videos, board games, home-video cassettes, and video games.

However, this is no longer a phenomenon indigenous to the United States. In addition to multiple products and audience segmentation, toy manufacturers and program production companies have expanded into the foreign markets. Often, motion pictures have simultaneous release in the international market as well as the United States, and the Care Bears, the Teenage Mutant Ninja Turtles, the Trolls, and the Lion King become a part of the world ("Global Ads," 1984; "Tip-Top Trolls," 1992; Groves, 1994).

7

♦♦♦

International Expansion

In addition to expanding markets within the United States, those in the business of children's entertainment have begun to recognize the potential of the international marketplace. Production deals are negotiated, movies are released, and television and toys are increasingly available to a global audience. The Walt Disney Company develops coproduction agreements with Scottish and Australian television, Nickelodeon sets up European distribution, and ABC/DIC brings *C.O.W. Boys of Moo Mesa* to Chinese television. Meanwhile, *The Lion King* is released concurrently in the United States, South America, South Africa, and Israel. He-Man toys and cartoons are available in over 30 countries; a full complement of ThunderCats merchandise is for sale in Britain's BBC Stores; *Sesame Street,* broadcast in over 115 counties, has 500 internationally licensed products. And the Teenage Mutant Ninja Turtles are everywhere.

This internationalization of children's entertainment is not new. Licensed versions of *Howdy Doody* merchandise and the program were available in Canada and Mexico, and Hanna–Barbera and Disney cartoons have long been a part of the international marketplace. However, these alliances were primarily the sale of an American product to a foreign market. Now, such arrangements are designed to transcend national boundaries and borders.

Chapter 6 addressed one way in which those involved in children's entertainment sought to expanded their financial base through audience segmentation and multiple outlets. This chapter will look at another, the aggressive move into international markets. Neither is unique to the 1990s, but in the past, they were a supplementary source of revenue; now, they are central to decision making and financial success.

International arrangements are based on shared investments and corporate design as global distribution overlays organizational decisions. This is best represented by two organizations: Zodiac Entertainment and their characters Widget, Mr. Bogus, and Twinkle; and Saban Entertainment's Power Rangers. Zodiac Entertainment was one of the first U.S. organizations to develop *original* characters—Mr. Bogus, Widget, and Twinkle—for an international market, exemplifying this trend toward a global product.[1] Saban Entertainment brought together bits of Japanese action film and U.S. characters to create *Mighty Morphin Power Rangers*, distributed in over 70 countries.

Again, the focus here is on commercial children's television, but other media products cannot be ignored. According to one report: "Recorded music (e.g., CDs, cassettes, and vinyl records) produced in the United States is among the most listened-to music in the world" (U.S. Department of Commerce, 1993, p. 20). Between 1989 and 1991, U.S. export of these products rose 47%; net export (the percent exports exceed imports) rose slightly more than 50% (U.S. Department of Commerce, 1993, p. 21). These figures are not available for children's products but, given the market trends, there is no reason to believe that the rise in exports would not apply to children's media too.

American videocassettes and motion pictures are also popular in other countries. Within 2 weeks of its release, *The Lion King* had sold 2.88 million tickets in 11 countries (Groves, 1994). Another popular children's film, *Home Alone 2: Lost in*

New York, ranked in the top 10 of several countries shortly after its release ("Back Page," 1993). Table 7.1 demonstrates the popularity of other child-oriented movies in select countries.

In 1993, *Home Alone 2: Lost in New York* and *Beauty and the Beast* were ranked as the top-10 most popular films, based on box-office revenue in 10 countries.

FOREIGN MARKETS: TELEVISION PROGRAMMING

American children's programming is an important commodity in the international market for a number of reasons. Among them are the growing population of young people and the heavy reliance on animation for children's entertainment. A review of the world population indicates that most countries are experiencing, or predicted to experience, a rise in population similar to that in the United States (Department of International Economic and Social Affairs, 1991, pp. 4–9). This suggests an increasing demand for product. A U.S. Department of Commerce Report stated that "many of the [media] products in demand in the United States soon become popular with young audiences worldwide, which watch the United States intently for the latest pop culture trend"

TABLE 7.1. International Box Office, Top-Ten-Ranked Motion Pictures Based on Box-Office Revenue, January 1993

	Movie and rank			
Country	Home Alone 2	Beauty and the Beast	Snow White	Honey, I Blew Up the Kids
Australia	3			8
Brazil	1		6	
France	8			
Germany	8	5		
Holland	6	4		
Italy		5		
Japan	2			
South Africa	4	9		8
UK/Ireland	3			

Note. Data compiled from *Variety Europe,* reprinted in "Back Page" (1993, p. 152).

(U.S. Department of Commerce, 1993, p. 51). This report identified several other reasons for the increased demand for U.S. media products: Linguistic differences are mitigated as the English-speaking population grows, and where data are available on the subject, leisure time is increasing universally (pp. 49–50). Also, animation translates well to foreign markets: It relies on stylized characters and generic time that require minimal cultural interpretation. Programs as disassociated from reality as *Popeye, He-Man and the Masters of the Universe,* and *Bugs Bunny* or quintessentially American programs like *The Teenage Mutant Ninja Turtles* are successful on the international market (Frankel, 1986; Bennett, 1991; Paxman, 1996, p. 104).

In the past, the international distribution of U.S. children's programming was restricted by the number of television outlets available in foreign markets; often these markets had quotas on nonindigenous material further limiting demand. Changes in technology allowing for satellite distribution that crosses national boundaries, the increase in commercial options, and the addition of cable have fueled a demand for programming in the foreign market. In the U.S. market, that demand was satisfied with children's programming; the same has occurred in other countries. In the European market, the changes in technology and corresponding increase in distribution outlets, along with an era of deregulation, have led to new services such as Kindernet in the Netherlands, Canal J in France, and the European Children's Channel. American companies represented by Worldvision and Turner Program Services, and cable companies such as Nickelodeon, the Disney Channel, and the Cartoon Channel, recognized these new markets and have moved into foreign distribution more aggressively.

These changes are not Eurocentric. Though Japan has allowed very little foreign broadcast programming to date, during the 1990s, thirty new stations are expected in the Japanese market based on satellite and cable technology (Kilburn, 1991). In the early 1990s, Thailand approved five new television stations, two privately owned and three in the public-service tradition (Blaufarb, 1992). Situations such as these will create a further demand for programming and, no doubt, much of that demand will be met by the growing children's export market.

Table 7.2, based on a survey of stations conducted by Television Business International (TBI), illustrates the distribution of American children's programming in many countries during the early 1990s.

Of the 20 countries responding to the TBI survey, only Japan and The Netherlands reported that at the time of the survey they did not purchase programming from the United States. Overall, the 20 countries represent 50 stations or networks. Excluding the three nonreporting networks (ARD/Germany, Italia 1, Rete 4/Italy) and the six U.S. networks represented (Cartoon, Nickelodeon, ABC, CBS, NBC, PBS), 29 reporting networks use at least some U.S. children's programming. Over 50% of the imported programming is represented by the English-language countries—United States, Canada, United Kingdom, Australia, New Zealand. Conversely, none of the U.S. networks report using imported programming. By 1995, this began to change as the U.S. public broadcasting stations and some cable stations began importing international programming. For example, in 1995, the Cartoon Network introduced *Small Worlds,* an hour of international films.

New outlets, like those that will be available in Japan and Thailand, mean a greater demand for programming and U.S. organizations with large libraries are well-positioned to meet that demand. But the demand is not just for programming; an opportunity for merchandising is also created. Retail goods and media products are a part of the package. Speaking about *The Hanna–Barbera Hour,* a representative of Worldvision, the distribution company for Hanna–Barbera, stated, "[Hanna–Barbera's international program] was put together to open up the marketplace for tie-ins, and to bring the corporate profile of Hanna–Barbera to the world, as well as the individual characters" (Bill Peck, U.K. Managing Director, Worldvision, in Dawtrey, 1991, p. 522).

TABLE 7.2. Imported Children's Programming, Amount of Hours and Source of Programming, Early 1990s

Country	Channel or network	Total hours per week	Hours imported	Supplying country
Australia	ABC	23.5	875	Canada, US, UK
	Nine	10.5	Varies	US
	Seven	26	250	US
Austria	ORF	14		Germany, US, UK
Belgium	RTBF	5	152	France, UK, US, Canada, Germany
	BRTN	9.5	276	US, Canada, UK, New Zealand, Europe
Canada	CBC	12		US/Canada
	CTV	1	0	
Denmark	DR	8.3		Worldwide
	TV2	8	250	US, UK
Finland	MTV	3	150	US
	YLE (TV2)	3		US, UK, Australia, Poland, Czech
	YLE (FST)	5.5	90	UK, Holland, Canada, Germany
France	France 2	5.75		Europe, Canada, US
	Canal J	93	3,400	Canada
	France 3	123		US, Europe, Canada
Germany	ARD[a]	6.3		
	Premiere	10	180	France, UK, US
	Pro 7	25		US, Canada, Europe, Japan
	RTL Plus	12	500	US, Japan
	ZDF	9	55	UK, Canada, Scandinavia
Italy	Italia[a] 1	31.3		
	Rete 4	6.3		
	Junior TV	56	2,000	UK, Japan, Europe, Australia
	Rai 2	6.3		US, Europe

(continued)

TABLE 7.2. *(continued)*

Country	Channel or network	Total hours per week	Hours imported	Supplying country
Japan	Fuji TV	8.5	6–12	UK, Spain
	NTV	6	0	
	TV Asahi	8	0	
	TBS[a]	2.5	0	
Luxembourg	RTL4	15		US
Netherlands	Kindernet	21	250	France, UK, Germany, Australia
New Zealand	TVNZ	40		US, UK, Australia
Portugal	RTP[a]	31		UK, US, France, Australia
	TVI	7	450	US, UK, Europe
Spain	Antena 3	21	675	US, Japan, Spain, Europe
	RTVE[a]	28	700	US, France
	Tele5[a]	33	514	US, Japan, Europe
Sweden	SVT	3	Varies	Canada, US, Japan
Switzerland	TSI	7	150	UK, US, Italy
	TSR	11	260	Europe, US
UK	BBC	20		US, Canada, Germany
	BSkyB	31.5		US, France
	TCC[a]	91	2,800	Worldwide
	ITV	11.2	27	US
US	Cartoon	168		
	Nickelodeon	100	6	UK
	ABC[a]	5		
	CBS[a]	4		
	NBC	2.5	0	
	PBS	26		

Note. Data from the TBI Global Children's Programming and Animation Survey (September 1993, pp. 54–57).
[a]Some data are based on estimates.

As the landscape of foreign broadcasting changes, American companies stand ready to bring in program and product and so *The Teenage Mutant Ninja Turtles* are introduced in Britain, Germany, Japan, Singapore, and Malaysia as a toy and media event.

FOREIGN MARKETS: MERCHANDISE

James McNeal, an authority on children's consumerism, identified several arguments for expanding the toy market into the international market.

1. Ninety percent of the population of families and 75% of the family incomes are outside the United States.
2. In the United States, toy manufacturers are sharing a well- worked market; other countries offer new possibilities.
3. Competition is not strong in other countries, making them vulnerable to the aggressive strategies of the United States.
4. Often American goods such as McDonald's restaurants, Barbie dolls, and Coca-Cola are favored over indigenous products.
5. Children's preferences are not well established, in general, making them more vulnerable. (McNeal, 1992, pp. 230–231)

Increasingly, based on this strategy and the growing world youth population, overseas distribution of children's retail merchandise and licensing agreements has become a part of the television package. Brian Lacey, while Director of Market Development at Zodiac Entertainment, claimed licensing agreements are central to the negotiations for foreign program distribution (Lacey, 1992).[2]

Consequently, the international toy market is beginning to reflect the changes in the U.S. market with licensed products, program-based concepts, and shifting retail patterns. Hanna–Barbera developed the international version of *The Hanna–Barbera Hour,* featuring Hanna–Barbera characters "to bring the corporate profile of Hanna–Barbera to the world, as well as the individual characters" for merchandising (Dawtrey, 1991). The Smurfs, He-Man, and ThunderCats all had success in the international toy market (McClorey, 1984, p. S-52; Loftus, 1987). Toys 'R' Us not only changed the way toys were sold in the United States, but the company also brought the same "advantages" to parents in countries such as Japan, and Canada, and the Middle

East, Asia, and Europe. The store brought to these countries high volume, low prices, and U.S. toys ("Brawls in Toyland," 1992; Mehegan, 1990; "Toys 'R' Us," 1994). Companies such as Mattel and Hasbro became well established in foreign markets: 50% of Mattel's sales in 1991 were in 100 overseas markets (Schine & McWilliams, 1992).

Another incentive for international expansion is potential market size: The United States has 40 million children under age 10; Europe has 71 million; Latin America has 113 million; and the Soviet Union has 55 million children under the age of 10 (Mehegan, 1990). At present, the average dollar amount spent on children in other countries is less than in the United States, offering the toy manufacturers new market potential, as described by McNeal. As the media market grows, new television opportunities will help reach those children.

COPRODUCTIONS

In addition to changes discussed earlier, media industries have furthered economic stability by establishing coproduction agreements with companies in other countries. Coproduction arrangements can be defined at two levels of financial involvement. The first level is represented by arrangements designed to open up a market through the circumvention of national quotas. Local programming is made, based on an American model with American financing. This arrangement is represented by Disney studio's joint venture with, for example, Scottish Television (Guider, 1989). Episodes of *The Disney Club* are produced with a local host and audience, interspersed with segments from American versions of the program.

The second level of arrangement involves international financing to develop mutually beneficial characters. Here, a new program is produced, for both the U.S. and international market, with foreign investors. This arrangement is represented by the alliance between Thames Television and Nickelodeon. In 1987, the two companies entered into a coproduction agreement for *Count Duckula* ("KidVid Going International", 1988; "Viacom Executives," 1989). This was an animated program based on the success of, and similar to,

Thames Television's cartoon series *Dangermouse* that was distributed on Nickelodeon.

At these two levels, the institutional model presented in Chapter 4 (Figure 4.4) has not changed. The players simply have a different currency and passport. These particular coproduction arrangements involve the distribution of resources but not a sharing of culture. Although *The Disney Club* may have variations in musical themes and host-patter, Donald Duck is still up to the same old tricks, only now he does them on Scottish television and *Count Duckula* may be produced in the United Kingdom, but his spirit is American.

There is, however, a third level of coproduction arrangement that, although it is also centered in the Hollywood marketplace, offers interesting consequences for program content. Here, the intent is to create a program primarily for an international market. The object is to make the program intelligible to children from diverse backgrounds and cultures. As seen in Figure 7.1, these agreements do not shift the configuration of the model, the players do not change, but the playing field includes an

FIGURE 7.1. Market exchange in commercial broadcasting, international market, 1990s. Adapted from Melody (1973). Copyright 1973 by Yale University Press. Adapted by permission.

international component. Market strategy is driven by attempts to appeal to a global economy.

In all three configurations of these coproduction arrangements, the bond between advertiser and producer is still strong. Like the 1950s and the American version of *The Mickey Mouse Club,* European coproductions of *The Disney Club* serve to promote the Euro Disney theme park and Mickey Mouse T-shirts; Nickelodeon conveys brand awareness. Given the commercial nature of many of the new systems, advertisers still strive to reach the young audience. However, there is a new element to the model noted above: the International Agent.

As the foreign market for children's programming opens, it allows for the entrance of new players. In some instances, companies that cannot compete against established production houses, such as Zodiac Entertainment, have the opportunity to enter the rapidly expanding international market.

Zodiac Entertainment

Zodiac is an interesting alternative to other production houses discussed here for two reasons: (1) The U.S. company was financed primarily by foreign investments; and (2) the characters were designed for the global market. In the mid-1980s when the U.S. market was strong and international companies were looking for investment opportunities, representatives of Central Television, a British broadcasting and production house, met with Brian Lacey and Peter Keefe to discuss "possibilities." The result of that meeting was Zodiac Entertainment, a Central Television investment concentrating on children's entertainment. Recognizing the difficulty of competing against Disney and Fox for the U.S. children's market, Zodiac looked to the international arena. According to Lacey, because of a changing broadcast economy opportunities in the global market increased for small companies. Zodiac, founded in 1989, was the first production company that defined itself as a *global* corporation marketing children's programs and merchandise to the world market (Lacey, 1992).

Zodiac's programs, *Widget, Mr. Bogus,* and *Twinkle, the Dream Being,* had wide-ranging international distribution. *Wid-*

get was available in Brazil, Germany, Australia, Mexico, Italy, France, Spain, Greece, Portugal, Turkey, Taiwan, Malaysia, Singapore, Thailand, New Zealand, all Arabic speaking countries, and 80% of the U.S. market (Dawtrey, 1992; "Word on *Widget,*" 1992).

Zodiac, and Central Television, began with *Warp Rider,* a live-action teen soap that was a coproduction arrangement between Zodiac/Central Television and other foreign investors. Like the Disney agreements, the program was to be produced in one country with the cast from another. In this case, a French broadcaster was sharing productions costs and providing a cast for the French version ("Zodiac Entertainment," 1989; "Zodiac to Develop," 1989). Their next venture was *Widget the Whale Watcher,* a half-hour animated program with strong presales commitments from the foreign market before it went into production ("Zodiac to Develop," 1989).

Widget (1989), *Mr. Bogus* (1991) and *Twinkle* (1993) were Zodiac's three primary programs. Each of the characters was an original concept developed by those at Zodiac, allowing the company to maintain creative and legal control and to retain ancillary rights.

Financed by Britain's second-largest commercial program producer, Central Television, Zodiac had coproduction arrangements with the Korean Broadcasting System (KBS), and Korea's leading animation company (McClellan, 1992). In addition to the investment of Central Television, Zodiac developed coproduction arrangements with KBS and Sei Young through KBS Media Enterprises, a subsidiary of KBS established to invest in international program arrangements. For its investment, KBS was to receive exclusive rights to the programs in Korea, mainland China, Taiwan, Indonesia, Hong Kong, and Thailand. KBS and Sei Young also shared in merchandising rights to the show. This coproduction arrangement gave distribution and merchandising rights in Asia to Sei Young and an assurance of timely completion and quality animation to Zodiac. A similar coproduction arrangement was negotiated with MBC, a Korean commercial network, and Sei Young for *Mr. Bogus,* in which the Korean companies received

10% of the net profits from worldwide television licensing and merchandising sales (McClellan, 1992). *Twinkle the Dream Being,* Zodiac's final product, was the result of the Korean companies approaching Zodiac; here, MBC and Sei Young maintained primary rights, with Zodiac receiving full financing and about 35% of worldwide licensing and merchandising fees, excluding Korea (McClellan, 1992).

As demonstrated in Figure 7.2, the links between agencies reflected Zodiac Entertainment's involvement.

This model reflects Zodiac's involvement in all stages of production and distribution, with more limited involvement in *Twinkle, the Dream Being.* It also reflects the move to a global economy, with financing from the United Kingdom. and coproduction deals with Korean broadcasters and animation houses.

Twinkle, Zodiac's third character is an interesting example of more recent trends in character licensing. The icon of Twinkle began life as the symbol for an international trade exposition, with no links to children's entertainment or merchandising. The exposition organizers approached Sei Young to produce a cartoon show, based on the character, promoting the event (Lacey, 1992). Sei Young turned to Zodiac to develop and market the concept. Zodiac gave the icon a history and story.

The Zodiac stars were created as cultural characters in a generic land. Widget is a purple space alien sent to Earth to help solve problems. He can change shapes at will—he's prosocial and hip. His programs, recommended by the National Education Association, are considered FCC-friendly. Mr. Bogus started life as a claymation image. Zodiac acquired all rights to the image and gave him the personality of a "whimsical gremlin . . . who dwells in the nooks and crannies of a home, wreaking havoc on its unsuspecting human inhabitants" ("Really 'Bogus,' " 1990, p. 30). Rumor has it that Mr. Bogus is the reason socks disappear on laundry day.

Widget and Twinkle stories offer a prosocial message for children and story lines that promote themes of cultural harmony and personal integrity (McClellan, 1992). The distinction between these and other licensed characters is that

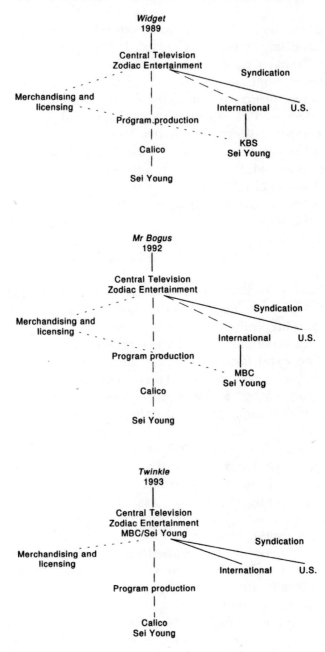

FIGURE 7.2. *Widget, Mr. Bogus, Twinkle,* global distribution, 1989–1993.
- - - - - - contractual links; ———— in-house control; – – – – –
coproduction agreements

Twinkle, Bogus, and Widget all were begun as icons with no history, personality, or citizenship, but with the intent to market them as entertainment and merchandise across cultures. The Smurfs come from the tradition of elves, He-Man from myth, and the Disney stable consists of anthropomorphic mice and ducks. The Zodiac characters are generic formulations created with the international market in mind. For example, there are no alpha or numeric characters in the *Widget* programs on the assumption that using linguistic symbols would assign an identifiable culture to the land.

Widget, Mr. Bogus, and *Twinkle, the Dream Being* were moderately successful programs in the U.S. syndication market, as well as having strong placement in the international market. Like other animated characters, Widget and Mr. Bogus are also available as licensed products, though the success of character licensing in the United States has been limited because, according to Lacey, the playing field is not level. Without the support of a Disney, Mattel, or Hasbro, it is difficult to establish a merchandising base. In many U.S. markets, the programs were placed in less desirable early-morning hours while Disney and other established syndicated programming blocks are found in the more commercially profitable afternoon hours (Freeman, 1994). However, in the international retail market the characters have had some success and could be found on T-shirts, posters, and pajamas.

In 1993, Central Television merged with another British company, Carlton Communications, and by January 1994, Zodiac Entertainment was no longer involved in the production of first-run, syndicated children's programming. The fact that Zodiac characters had only a moderate showing in the licensing and merchandising arena and Zodiac Entertainment did not have the "deep pockets" of a Disney or Hanna–Barbera made it difficult for them to compete in the marketplace, domestic or international.

Saban Entertainment

Saban Entertainment is another independent company considered important in the international market. Like Zodiac,

Saban is an independent company with the international market as its objective. Whereas Zodiac Entertainment attempted to offer an alternative to the major companies, Haim Saban's goal is to become another Disney, with theme parks, television shows, toys, movies, and gym and Karate schools (Freeman, 1993).

Saban Entertainment is among the largest producers and distributors of children's programs with international interests. Founded in 1983, Saban has strong coproduction links with a number of foreign companies including Toei Company, a Japanese production company, and CLT, a Luxembourg broadcast company (Freeman, 1993).

Saban Entertainment's library has over 2,000 programs including *Sweet Valley High*, a program based on a very popular series of teen books. One of their most successful programs was built around the live-action children's program, *Mighty Morphin Power Rangers*. Although the program was banned in some countries because of violent content, at one point it could be found on television in over 100 markets, including Australia, Belgium, France, Germany, Greece, Italy, The Netherlands, Portugal, Spain, and the United Kingdom (Freeman, 1993).

The Mighty Morphin Power Rangers is a half-hour, live-action[3] program about six high-school students who "morph" into heroes to fight the evil villain in the tradition of superheroes. Except for the fact that it is live-action, the program is similar to many animated action-adventure programs that feature multiple characters. Jason, Zack, Trini, Kimberly, Billy, and Tommy live in a town called Angel Grove and, like He-Man and the ThunderCats, with a magical incantation, they become THE MIGHTY MORPHIN POWER RANGERS. Using their brains and martial arts skills they, too, fight evil. Sold separately, of course. Saban retains control over all aspects of media and merchandising, both in the domestic and international market, including merchandising arrangements (Freeman, 1993).

Building on the success of other multiple-character, action-adventure programs, the *Mighty Morphin Power Rangers* is a derivative of *sentai*, superhero teams, a genre that is popular in Japan. The idea was imported by Haim Saban when he came across *Zyu Rangers,* a *sentai* produced by Toei, in which five Japanese teens "morphed into spandex-suited super-heroes" (Katz, 1994, p. 8). Saban brought the idea back to the United States, replaced the Japanese actors with Americans and, using the action sequences from the Toei Company productions, created the *Mighty Morphin Power Rangers.*

Videocassettes and interactive stories on CD-Rom are produced by Saban, and the motion picture is from 20th Century Fox studios. Licensing fees brought in over $2.5 million in 1993; pre-Christmas sales of the action figure alone that year were $1 million (Freeman, 1993). The show's success matches or exceeds that of *He-Man and the Masters of the Universe, ThunderCats,* and the *Teenage Mutant Ninja Turtles.*

As is evident from Figure 7.3, the relationship of those involved in the process of creating the Power Rangers is more direct than in any of the arrangement discussed previously.

In Figure 7.3, all roads lead to Saban Entertainment. This model demonstrates the increasing strength between corporations and international coproduction agreements. Saban Entertainment's only contractual link is with Fox Television. All other aspects are either in-house or coproduction arrangements. Fox Television provides a strong audience and access

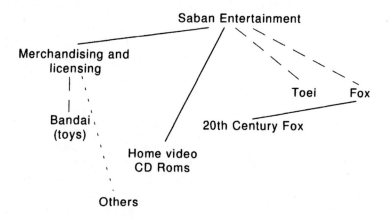

FIGURE 7.3. *Mighty Morphin Power Rangers,* Saban Entertainment, 1994. - - - - - - - contractual links; ——————— in-house control; – – – – – – coproduction agreements.

to 20th Century Fox for movie production, and Toei Company, one of the major Japanese media corporations, provides lower upfront risk (Freeman, 1993) as well as the special-effects segments and production support in return for distribution in the Asian market.

What makes Zodiac and Saban most relevant to this discussion is their international focus. Those involved in Zodiac Entertainment understood the importance of *Widget* in the context of the international marketplace. In part, their decision was pragmatic—Disney, Fox, and Warner Bros. dominated the domestic marketplace for children's programming—but the decision was also made in the belief that, to be financially viable, a company had to compete in the global market. Haim Saban approaches children's programming from much this same position. Claiming the world to be "one big boundaryless marketplace" he is quoted as saying:

> We have this picture puzzle of various countries around the world with each being able to generate a certain amount of money for certain products. And if we can make sense out of a production by mixing Korean and Luxembourgish investment that would cover the production costs, then the rest of the world is open for sales. (Freeman, 1993, p. 30)

No longer are limits of the marketplace defined by national boundaries; rather, the global market is considered foremost in decisions about program production and distribution, motion picture release, and the marketing of toys and merchandise.

As foreign broadcast systems begin to resemble the multichannel environment of the commercial U.S. system, demand for product will continue to rise. Consequently, there will be a need for programming and, if predictions hold true, that programming will be children's entertainment from the United States. However, with these arrangements come a negotiation for merchandising and toys as the world becomes a "boundaryless marketplace," both in terms of the elimination of national boundaries and the ubiquity of children's material culture. Toys, T-shirts, and pajamas are a part of the trade for program entertainment worldwide.

But what does it mean to a world raised on the *Mighty Morphin Power Rangers* or *Widget?* Will we, at one level, develop a common language, or will we lose a cultural richness as indigenous stories are replaced by Hollywood fantasy?

8
♦♦♦
Consequences

This book began with the statement that culture is

> a whole body of beliefs, practices, and material artifacts.
> . . . [It] is commercial because of the central place material
> goods and reminders of material goods have in it. But the
> term "commercial culture" can be used in another sense as
> well, when applied to the flow of ideas and expressions that
> shape our national character and outlook. (Bogart, 1991,
> p. 2)

Underlying this is the assumption that particular economic
systems make it easier for some "material goods and remind-
ers" to succeed and others not. In the business of children's
entertainment, success has come to those who can transcend
boundaries: large corporations with deep pockets that can
move across international boundaries and into alternative
media markets.

Children's entertainment has become defined by profitability. Companies with the resources of a Disney or Mattel
succeed; Zodiac does not: The commercial model governs the
process, and Disney rules the domain. Small islands of creativity exist on public broadcasting and in places such as
Nickelodeon, or with independent companies that find a

niche in the video or music or book industry, but mostly the air is filled with Mickey Mouse or the character *du jour*.

Although the intent here has been to demonstrate the economic links between production and entertainment, the material culture, the ideological nature of the media industries, cannot be ignored, for the media are more than products of leisure, they are also products of culture: *the flow of ideas and expressions that shape our national character and outlook*. Children (and adults) learn about the world through the media. They are new to all this and learn not only through experience, but also through the stories they are told. The material culture represented by the media cultivates a way of thinking, consumption and the acquisition of "things" is encouraged, and particular assumptions about the world are promoted.

Our children learn to equate happiness with trips to McDonald's. Attending the movies is not a simple experience but an event re-lived through an array of coloring books, computer games, and pajamas. Toys demand less imagination when the generic teddy bear is replaced by a Lion King who comes with a history by Disney. Although stories are still about good versus evil, the tenor changes when cartoon characters bring quick fixes to problems that are solved in 30 minutes, with time for commercials. The shopping mall is the playground, and the video is the storyteller.

We have found that character licensing and product tie-ins are not new. Campbell Soup dolls, Davy Crockett hats, and Roy Rogers ensembles all predate the introduction of what is called product-based programming, licensing, and merchandising entertainment. Like our child of the 1990s, a child of the 1930s could wear a Mickey Mouse shirt and carry a Shirley Temple doll; a child of the 1950s could dress in a Dale Evans skirt and carry a Toni doll. At first glance, it would not seem such a long way from Bobby Benson's ranch. In each case, the child is a consumer primed to take part in the economy and encouraged to want "things"—to consume goods and services in a disposable world. What has happened more recently is the acceleration of the process and the takeover of all aspects of children's play and imagination. Children are exposed to the consumer world at a dizzying pace. Borders between storytelling and advertising and worldly possessions blur. What are the consequences of a world immersed in the commercialism of *The Lion King* or the violence of *Mortal Kombat?*

The consumerization of the child is extraordinarily complex; their toys and media, and even their G.I. Joe underwear become a part of the material culture and the "ideas and expressions that shape [a] national character and outlook" (Bogart, 1991, p. 2). With the consumerization of the child comes the ideological shaping of the adult. That is not to say we will all demand our Lion King as adults, though several recent commercials play on the child within, but we will come to expect life to play out in particular ways.

This book has set out the economic circumstances that have led to this shift. Children in the United States have long had income and influence over family purchases, but children are now treated as a market segment, consumers in their own right. Advertisers and marketers address children as they do adults with money to spend "for whatever they want to, whenever they want to, wherever they want to" (McNeal, 1992, p. 34).

The child market, as we know it today, is a result of the growing complexity of the marketplace.

An analysis of the *Smurfs, He-Man and the Masters of the Universe,* and the *ThunderCats* demonstrates the increasingly self-serving corporate deals and the economic decisions generated by a recognition that the status between consumer and audience has become less clear. Large corporations develop subsidiaries designed to serve the young market, further evidence that there is a rationale for investment. The shift from a public-interest philosophy to a deregulated marketplace allows for a climate of economic expedience. An examination of the connections between these makes obvious the contradictions between groups. On the one hand, interest groups such as Action for Children's Television are concerned with the special needs of the child, and, on the other, industry representatives are concerned with the maximization of the audience/consumer.

The idea of children as a "special" audience, though historically important to American culture, simply cannot be supported in an economic system that allows no consideration for public service. Government agencies, instituted to assure that the broadcasting industries would serve the public, have become increasingly dominated by industry. And commercial-length programs are the "logical" extension of a system that weds commerce and entertainment, with little regard for "the public interest, convenience, and necessity." Fundamentally, Mattel's He-Man is not so different from Hecker's Bar-O Ranch or Buster Brown Shoes, as all are the function of a system centered in profit rather than service.

In the meantime, the business of children's television expands into the business of children's entertainment, as what had previously been considered adult entertainment is now available to children.

An analysis of the industry demonstrates the increasingly self-serving corporate deals and economic decisions generated by a recognition that the status between consumer and audience has become less clear. Large corporations develop subsidiaries designed to serve the young market, furthering evidence that there is a rationale for investment. Companies such as Zodiac have international financing in what is seen as a "boundaryless marketplace."

Changes in technology have led to expansions in other markets where one story can become television, movie, audio-tape, videocassette, CD-Rom, software, and computer game. Finally, toy companies and media industries recognize that Europe, Southeast Asia, South America, and Japan offer populations of children who are ready to learn Barney's theme song, or demand their Nick Jr., or, like He-Man or the Power Rangers, call upon some magical powers to solve problems.

THE CHILDREN

The idea that children are a special group is neither new or different. This philosophy is rooted in the tradition of the U.S. reform movement of the early 1900s. An important function of the early reform movement was the protection of children and a concern for their special needs. As early as 1909, the entertainment industry was of particular concern:

> Is it not astounding that a city allows thousands of youth to fill their impressionable minds with these absurdities [motion picture tales] which certainly will become the foundation for their working moral codes and the data from which they will judge the proprieties of life? (Addams, 1972, pp. 79–80)

Similar concerns were expressed 60 years later:

> A three or four year old should be taught honesty and fair dealing, not suspicion and deceit. There is enough time to learn the sordid side of life after the age of 12. (Testimony by Action for Children's Television; Federal Communication Commission, 1970, p. 12)

However, each of these groups carry with them an acceptance of the basic economic system. For example:

> Never did [Jane Addams] carry her arguments to their logical conclusion and suggest that there was something fundamentally wrong with the industrial system. . . . The best she could offer was to help adjust young people to the system and make them a little happier in the process. (Davis, cited in Addams, 1972, pp. xxvii–xxviii)

Contemporary concerns about children are also rooted in "reform" not "revolution." The intention is not to do away with the capitalist system or the profit motive; rather, the intention is to make the system work in a preconceived ideology of good.

This concept of children as special has a noble tradition within U.S. culture. However, a capitalist system, one based on profit maximization, allows no room for subsuming the needs of a particular group. A history of the consumer market and the entertainment industry demonstrates that children are a market, no different than any other audience share. And when market productivity and profit maximization are the driving force behind industry decisions, contribution will be determined by advertising dollars and market shares, whether it is an audience for movie theaters or for television advertisers.

Increasingly, children have become defined as a marketable audience; therefore, because industry is not serving the interest of the child, it is argued that it is the government's responsibility to see that children's interests are protected. Congressional Hearings encourage the record industry, motion picture companies, and the producers of video games to set standards.

THE REGULATORS

In other countries, there is often a tradition of children as a special audience, and media that serves a public interest. Quotas on advertising, hours of programming, and special children's hours have not been unusual. In the United States, a different path was determined.

Early in its history, the Federal Communications Commission's mandate was to assure that the broadcast industry served the "public interest, convenience or necessity." The struggle between competing groups to define that phrase has been evident over the years, and nowhere are the contradictions more obvious than in the attempts to regulate children's television. Industry representatives consider government attempts to intervene in programming philosophies as in violation of First Amendment Rights, whereas activists consider intervention and regulation as the only way to protect the child from the materialist nature of the commercial system.

The 1990 Congress passed The Children's Television Act, and in 1996, the FCC set standards for the broadcasting industry based on the Act. Time will tell if these standards bring about change.

THE FUTURE

Prediction is best left to crystal balls and venture capitalists. When this project began, product-based programming had just become a concern. Although such programming no longer dominates as it did for a short time in the 1980s, it is now accepted as a part of children's media. At that time, children's radio did not exist, and children's books were generally found on a few shelves in the back of the bookstores. In 10 years, the children's market has exploded and the movie industry, radio, book, and computer manufacturers all consider children an important market force. And, although there has always been an international marketplace, sales to foreign countries are now central to the decision-making process. Such recognition may fluctuate, but as long as children have an expendable income, they will be defined, not as a special audience, but as a special market and therefore fair game.

Short of revolution, it would appear there is little we can do. However, it is our responsibility as adults to see that children are not discouraged from the true magic of the world but that we recognize storytelling has become a business.

As a nation, we must take responsibility for all children. It is important that we acknowledge the importance of childhood in our policies, our distribution of wealth and resources, and in our everyday decisions.

As an industry, we can do this by recognizing the nature of children and the way in which they see the world. We can offer them an array of adventures and stories that encourage creativity and curiosity. We can speak to their intellect and not their avarice, and we can recognize them as a special audience, not a consumer audience.

As caretakers—teachers, parents, aunts and uncles, neighbors, and friends—we must leave lines of communication open and listen to their worries and fears and interests. In our media environment, it is impossible, and not necessarily desirable, to protect them from the images of the world, but it is important that we listen to their stories too. Through conversations, we can gain insight into their understandings and help them interpret the world.

Notes

CHAPTER ONE

1. This history is based on a number of resources, both primary and secondary. Useful material included historical texts on the topic: for example, Grumbine's work in the 1930s. Because of their position and influence, the writings of people such as Gruenberg and Grumbine are considered important. In addition, *Parents' Magazine* and *Printer's Ink* were reviewed for contemporary views on the child as consumer. The trade magazine *Printer's Ink* is significant because of its importance as one of the primary resources for the advertising industry.

2. Nationally advertised data are used because they offer a standard of measure and are the most readily available. Very few records have been maintained on this information at the local level and, particularly, on children's entertainment. Table 1.1 is a listing of all programs categorized as "children," "daytime drama," or "daytime comedy" and the listed program sponsor. It is not a definitive list, because some programs were identified as having multiple or cooperative sponsorships, with no indication of the products. Many of the children's programs were locally produced, and the sponsorship of those are not known. However, there is no reason to doubt that those programs would be very different from the nationally distributed and sponsored shows. Grumbine's 1938 data, discussed earlier, included programs that children listened to

as well as radio programs for children; this list only includes daytime programming aimed at children.

3. This comment is particularly prophetic, as the expansion of seasonal items is the base of recent marketing decisions that have changed the toy industry.

4. The data discussed here are from an unpublished database of over 1,000 citations, collected on all academic research on children and the media published in books or journals in the United States. They are available from the author.

CHAPTER TWO

1. During the 1970s and 1980s, numerous hearings that addressed the kinds of programming and the amount of advertising on television were held in Washington, D.C. Occasionally, the broadcasters would be put on notice or there would be changes in the number of minutes of advertising allowed during "children's" programs. However, for the most part, children's television has been at the mercy of the political climate and there has never been any real change. In 1990 the "Children's Television Act" was passed by Congress in an attempt to circumvent the limited reform brought about by the Federal Communications Commission (FCC) or the Federal Trade Commission (FTC). As of late 1996, there appeared to be more available programming because of the Act, and many programs claimed to be "FCC Friendly."

2. The Prime-Time Access Rule and the Financial and Syndication Rulings were three of the major policy decisions that contributed to changes in the industry structure. And they are the most important to this discussion because of the impact on program production and distribution. However, the independent stations have also benefited from technological changes such as satellite and cable transmission, and FCC rulings aimed at cable transmission of signals (Must Carry).

3. To clarify the terms used here: In *barter or advertiser-supported* arrangements, the station exchanges commercial airtime rather than financial capital for programming. Programs are bartered for a percentage of commercial airtime, or alternatively, cash/barter arrangements are made where a combination of cash payment and some portion of the commercial airtime is exchanged. The most common arrangement at this writing is 2:4, with 2 minutes of time to the advertiser or distributor and 4 minutes remaining with the

station on a half-hour program. Programs, either previously aired on the networks or made for the syndication market, are licensed to a station. Often, in return, the agent that controls the rights to the show collects a certain amount of station advertising time (either within that particular program or another time) to sell to advertisers.

Syndication is the distribution process of licensing or granting the right to use programs on a station-by-station basis. It can be previously exhibited or recorded material such as motion pictures or network series (off-net), or the program can be made specially for syndication (first-run).

4. This history is based on a number of resources both primary and secondary. There are several useful resources on the history of network children's television (see, e.g., Grossman, 1980; Luke, 1990; Turow, 1981; Schneider, 1987). The history presented here is offered as background to the development of a child audience, not as a definitive history of children's television.

5. It should be noted that there is a difference between the network television industry, the local affiliated stations, and the independent local stations. This figure demonstrates the limited network audience on the weekday; there were less than 80 independent stations when Melody wrote this.

6. Animation was the preferred format, because the economic potential of animated programming is enhanced by the nature of the characters that makes them easy to replicate as toys; the fact that the cartoons can be recycled to a new audience in 3-year generations; and the simplistic drawings make them easy to dub for an international market.

7. The Disney Channel and Nickelodeon were available in the early 1980s, but at that point, cable was available to less than 8% of the television households (Sterling & Kittross, 1990); by 1993, 62% of the television households had cable ("Year in Review," 1994).

8. The figures for local programming in New York during 1970 are based on Turow's work (1981). The minutes of local children's programming on network and independent stations were added to his data to account for an the hour/week figure using *The New York Times* television listings January 11–17, 1970. The amount of available hours for 1990 was arrived at using his methodology and the New York metropolitan edition of *TV Guide*, October 20–26, 1990.

9. Like any economic relationship, sponsorship changes in the radio and television industry were the result of a complex set of conditions. For example, although the factors listed here—rising

production costs, increased competition, growth of profit from advertising—were all in place, others would suggest it was the quiz-show scandals of the late 1950s that drove these changes.

CHAPTER THREE

1. The attention here is on independent stations rather than network or network-affiliated broadcast stations because independents have traditionally programmed against the stronger afternoon network programming of soap operas with children's programming. The weekday cartoons have been a classic counterprogramming strategy used by the independents to provide alternative programming options in the competitive environment of broadcast television (Frazier Gross & Kadlec Inc., 1986).

2. The *industry* genealogy of the Care Bears is also of interest. They were introduced jointly by American Greeting Cards and General Mills based on the successful model of Strawberry Shortcake, with Kenner Toys as the barter agent.

3. In addition to Rainbow Brite, Twink and the 16 characters listed, the 1985 Mattel Toy catalog itemized 40 character items available in the Rainbow Brite line. And, of course, she is a media star with several feature-length films, home video cassettes, and television specials.

4. This advertisement ran in trade journals as diverse as *Chain Store Age* and *Variety*. It was on high-gloss, stiff board as a complex foldout. Clearly, much money went into the introduction of this new line of Care Bears.

5. Although the arrows are directional, causality is never so obvious.

CHAPTER FOUR

1. There were a number of examples of successful products/programs around; however, none had the overwhelming success on commercial television and in retail sales as the Smurfs.

2. It is always difficult to illustrate process with models. One implies praxis; the other is static. The attempt here is to catch the evolution of the media industries at particular points in time. The first is 1973, as modeled by Melody when networks were in control

of the market. Later models attempt to present shifts caught at a particular moment in history.

3. A master toy licensee has the right to sell a broad range of products in various categories; most licensing arrangements are for a specific product or design.

4. In February 1986, Telepictures merged with Lorimar to form Lorimar/Telepictures. The merger brought together production (Lorimar) and syndication (Telepictures).

5. The episode synopses are from a packet of readings and activities that Telepictures sent to grade schools for teachers to use as educational material.

6. In 1985, LJN was bought by MCA, bringing together a film and entertainment company with a toy company that had sales based on action and fashion dolls—Brooke Shields, Michael Jackson, Voltron, ThunderCats, E.T., the World Wrestling Federation, and The Mask.

7. The actual number of stations that participated in the profit-sharing arrangements was small. What is important is that it was considered and opened up new configurations of economic arrangements. Telepictures representatives saw it as a "natural extension" of barter; Action for Children's Television proponents saw it as blackmail. The number of stations that were granted one of the equity arrangements was about 34.

CHAPTER FIVE

1. Two arguments often emerge when comparing public broadcasting and Nickelodeon to commercial systems. The first, that the quality and intent of programming on public broadcasting and Nickelodeon is different from that of the commercial media, is not the issue here, because the focus is on economic relationships not program content. The second, that access to these services is limited, is important but also disregarded here. Though many do not have access to these outlets, the discussion here is at the level of those involved in the decision-making process. Audience numbers are important as an abstract concept.

2. In 1995, Walt Disney Company purchased the ABC network, shifting the balance of power in the television industry. However, our interest here is primarily Disney cable. So we will examine the company from 1983 to 1995, the years when Disney cable dominated its television investments.

3. In 1996, Disney and Mattel signed an exclusive arrangement where Mattel has a 3-year agreement to a "first look" at all Disney characters worldwide (Levin, 1996).

4. To parallel the discussion of Disney, we will also examine Nickelodeon for the years 1980–1994.

5. There are a number of recent histories on public television and the public service tradition: Avery (1993), Hoynes (1994), and Lashley (1992). Unfortunately, none of them addresses the role of children's programming.

6. There is some debate on the commercial nature of CTW and the merchandising of its characters. Some would argue that the profusion of *Sesame Street* characters and the *Sesame Street* retail shops that compete with the Disney and Warner Bros. stores for mall space makes CTW no more philanthropic than commercial production houses. Although the debate has merit, the issue is the not-for-profit status of the corporation.

7. One difficulty in the trend toward private companies is the limited access to financial data. The Lyons Group and Quality Family Entertainment are both private corporations; Lancit is a public corporation and must file financial reports. As private corporations, the Lyons Group and Quality Family Entertainment are not required to make financial data available.

8. In 1995, PBS announced that their logo would be available for licensing on appropriate children's products, with revenues reinvested in PBS ("Licensing Deal," 1995).

CHAPTER SIX

1. Selected winter issues of the Sears catalog (1933–1990) were used to examine the type of children's items available and their connections to the media industries. The 1933 catalog advertised generic dolls and cars, but it also promoted Mickey Mouse toys, watches, and clothing; Popeye mechanical toys; Buck Rogers watches, rocket ship, books, guns, costumes, and games; a Shirley Temple doll; and a Wrigley Chewing Gum truck.

2. Unit sales and figures for market share for books and other forms of media that are not advertiser supported have proven to be difficult to locate. In part, this is a consequence of the multiple distribution venues and the fact the audience is based on sales, not advertising dollars. Figures can be located for individual publishing houses, record companies, or videocassette sales, but an overall

market share for children's media is dependent on total sales in the industry. Because children's media are perceived to be a small part of the market, the numbers are not considered significant.

3. Trading cards are an interesting collector's item that has been a part of children's material culture since the turn of the century. As noted in an earlier chapter, they were first used to promote consumer household goods as a premium for children. The contemporary trading card industry is a big business, and most of the cards are inspired by comic books and television shows (Nashawaty, 1994). While buying comic books on a research trip to the local news shop, I heard the owner mention to a coworker that it was necessary to buy more X-Men cards. When queried by the intrepid researcher, she said it was the one item that she could not keep in stock: They literally fly out of the store. Nashawaty also comments on this phenomenon.

4. Anyone who has listened to children's music recently would disagree with this characterization. Some of the most interesting and innovative work is being done in this genre; however, it suffers from a perception of tinny sound and poor quality.

5. In the audio industry, *Billboard*'s figures for market share and sales are dependent on information from traditional record stores; children's records and cassettes can be found in a variety of retail outlets. As with books, sales for individual production houses are available, but this gives no information on the market share or the overall growth of the industry. However, all seem to agree that Disney is the dominant force in the audio and video market (e.g., Jeffrey, 1993).

6. After the introduction of television in the 1950s, the radio industry had little to do with the child audience. This began to change in the 1980s when, responding to the forces already identified as important to the growth of children's entertainment, the radio industry began to program for children. Among the first was WNYC in New York playing music of the *Smurfs* and *Sesame Street* with the stories of Hans Christian Andersen ("Children's Three Hours," 1984). This was followed by syndicated shows such as *Pickelberry Pie* and *Kidsamerica*; network programming represented by Kidwaves Radio Network, the Imagination Stations, and Radio AAHS; and child-format stations such as KPAL in Little Rock, Arkansas, KPLS in Los Angeles, and WWTC in Minneapolis.

Until 1993, it was difficult to determine radio's child audience because Arbitron, the primary source for audience ratings, did not collect data on children under 12. Radio AAHS became the first

Arbitron subscriber for these audience numbers (Cooper, 1993). The study found that 91% of all children under 12 listen to the radio, and for every two children listening, one adult is also in the audience.

In 1994, Fox Broadcasting began broadcasting FOX Kids Radio to a American and international radio markets. And in 1996, Disney entered the market.

CHAPTER SEVEN

1. Generally, international distribution, like domestic production, has depended on previously successful characters. For example, Nelvana of Canada imported of characters like Tintin (Belgium), Rupert Bear (Great Britain), and Babar (France) into the U.S. market. But generally these are *previously successful* characters unlike Zodiac's original characters.

Often animation is carried out by companies situated in foreign countries with low labor costs. This is not what is meant by "internationalization."

See Wildman and Siwek (1988) for an explanation of the international trade agreements in the adult media market.

2. Most of the information about Zodiac Entertainment comes from a personal interview with Brian Lacey, cofounder of the company, conducted in his New York City office, August 1992. Zodiac stopped production several years later, citing overwhelming competition from larger corporations. However, the company offers an interesting case study because of their attempts to transcend cultural boundaries.

3. The fact that this program is live-action and not animated contradicts many of the principles of children's programming. Animation allows for a timelessness and geographic anonymity that is usually not available in live-action; cartoon characters are less difficult to replicate; and, the stylized drawings allow for more possibilities—coyotes can fall off cliffs. However, the production techniques for the *Mighty Morphin Power Rangers* allow for many of these same possibilities.

References

Addams, J. (1972). *The spirit of youth and city streets.* Urbana: University of Illinois Press. (Reprint of 1909 edition)

Adler, R. (1980). Children's television advertising: History of the issue. In E. Palmer & A. Dorr (Eds.), *Children and the faces of television.* New York: Academic Press.

Ah-so many new cartoons to syndie TV. (February 13, 1985). *Variety,* 135.

American Greetings sees $250M in first year of Care Bears. (December 1982). *Playthings,* 54.

Arrington, C. (June 2, 1984). It's pumping plastic time as He-Man and his multimuscled minions rule toyland's battlefield. *People,* 106–107.

Association of National Advertisers, Inc., American Association of Advertising Agencies, Inc., American Advertising Federation. (November 24, 1978). *The positive case for marketing children's products to children.* New York: Authors.

Back Page: *Variety's* international box office. (May/June 1993). *Utne Reader,* 152.

Barcus, F. E. (1975). *Weekend commercial children's television.* Newtonville, MA: Action for Children's Television.

Battle of the fun factories. (December 16, 1985). *Time,* 44–46.

Bedford, K. (October 4, 1993). Posse chasing after purple cash cow. *Current,* 1.

Bennett, R. (January 1991). Animation bumps into cultural barriers. *The Hollywood Reporter,* S18.

Berry, J. (June 28, 1993). Wooing young consumers. *Publishers Weekly,* 35–37.

Beville, J. H. M. (1985). *Audience ratings.* Hillsdale, NJ: Erlbaum.

Big advertisers find Nickelodeon a darn good deal for the money. (April 5, 1989). *Variety,* 66.

Blatz, W. (January 1933). Train your child to take responsibility. *Parents' Magazine,* 14–15, 56.

Blaufarb, R. (August 10, 1992). Thais OK stations, but only two private. *Variety,* 32–33.

Blickstein, J. (June 1, 1992). From Turner to NBC: A change of channels. *Variety,* 49.

Block, R. (February 17, 1988). History of syndie, a short look back. *Variety,* 77.

Bogart, L. (March 1991). *The American media system and its commercial culture* (Occasional Paper No. 8). New York: Gannett Foundation Media Center.

Brawls in toyland. (December 21, 1992). *Business Week,* 36.

Bremmer, R. (Ed.). (1967). *Traps for the young.* Cambridge, MA: Harvard University Press.

Brodie, J., & Greene, J. (July 11–17, 1994). Dwarfs tell Disney: Draw! *Variety,* 1.

Brown, L. (June 1986). The law of unexpected consequences. *Channels,* 19.

Brown, P., & Fisher, M. (November 5, 1984). Big Bird cashes in. *Forbes,* 176, 178, 182.

Brown, R. (March 28, 1994). Nick to spend $30 million on kids. *Broadcasting and Cable,* 53.

Burroughs, R. (April 28, 1989). Books with easy hooks: Selling to the chains. *Publishers Weekly,* 37–42.

Butterfield Communications Group. (1986). *Barter Syndication: Four perspectives. Report prepared for the Association of Independent Television Stations and the Station Representatives Association.* Cambridge, MA: Author.

Cable castings: Disney doings. (February 15, 1988). *Broadcasting,* 123.

Care Bears: Advertisement. (September 1984). *Chain Store Age, General Merchandise Edition,* 53.

Carlson, M. (January–February 1986). Babes in toyland. *American Film,* 57.

Carter, B. (March 21, 1994). A cable challenger for PBS as king of the preschool hill. *New York Times,* 1.

Character licensing: Mickey Mouse, yes—Shirley Temple, no. (December 1970). *Playthings, 1,* 50–51, 106–107.

Children's programs in syndication. (August 15, 1977). *Television/Radio Age,* 24.

Children's three hours. (January 30, 1984). *Broadcasting.*

Clout! (December 21, 1992). *Business Week,* 66–73.

CO Films shelling $2.5-mil to push new 'Care Bears.' (August 5, 1987). *Variety,* 6–7.

Cole, B., & Oettinger, M. (1978). *Reluctant regulators: The FCC and the broadcast audience.* Reading, MA: Addison-Wesley.

Coleco Industries, Inc. (1986). *Annual report.* West Hartford, CT: Author.

Collins, L. (November 3, 1986). 'Thundercats' success no accident. *Advertising Age,* 25.

Cooper, J. (August 23, 1993). Arbitron to measure children's radio. *Broadcasting and Cable,* 52.

Cox, D. (January 23–29, 1995). Scholastic makes the grade in Hollywood. *Variety,* 13, 30.

Croghan, L. (August 21, 1994). A children's TV production company grows. *The New York Times,* 5.

CTW sees record licensing income. (August 25, 1975). *Advertising Age,* 16.

Darlin, D. (April 12, 1993). Highbrow hype. *Forbes,* 126–127.

Davey, G. W. (1926). *The chick that never grew up: A Bon Ami story.* Kansas City, MO: Faultless Starch/Bon Ami Co. (Reprinted 1983)

Dawson, V. (February 2, 1987). He-Man: The heroes' welcome. *The Washington Post,* C1.

Dawtrey, A. (January 1991). Europeans strive to overcome U.S. edge in animation. *The Hollywood Reporter,* S22, S52–S53.

Dawtrey, A. (September 28, 1992). ITV: The gap keeps growing. *Variety,* 30.

deCordova, R. (1994). The Mickey in Macy's window. In E. Smoodin (Ed.), *Disney discourse.* New York: Routledge.

Dempsey, J. (February 29, 1984). Barter-syndie may hit $500 mil in '84. *Variety,* 29.

Dempsey, J. (March 27–April 2, 1995). Family feature films get a familiar ring. *Variety,* 1, 91.

Department of International Economic and Social Affairs. (1991). *The sex and age distributions of population.* New York: United Nations.

Diamond, D. (June 13, 1987). Is the toy business taking over kid's TV? *TV Guide,* 4–8.

Doan, R. (August 23, 1969). For hire: An electronic nanny. *TV Guide,* 24–25.

Dugan, I. J. (November 4, 1996). The thing that ate the kids' market. *Business Week,* 174–176.

Edwards, E. (June 29, 1994). Head of PBS answers critics. *The Washington Post,* D6.

Elkind, D. (1981). *The hurried child.* Reading, MA: Addison-Wesley.

Englehardt, T. (September 1986). Saturday morning: The hard sell takeover of kids TV. *Mother Jones,* 38–28, 54.

Englehardt, T. (1987). The Shortcake strategy. In T. Gitlin (Ed.), *Watching television.* New York: Pantheon Press.

Every child needs an allowance. (March 1930). *Parents' Magazine,* 18–19, 38, 40.

Ewen, S. (1988). *All consuming images.* New York: Basic Books.

Farhi, P. (November 29, 1989). Disney's new fantasy. Adult music. *The Washington Post,* C4.

Federal Communications Commission. (July 27, 1978). 68 FCC 2d 1344. *Second Notice of Inquiry.*

Federal Communications Commission. (April 29, 1970). Docket No. 19142. *Reply Comments of Action for Children's Television.*

Federal Communications Commission. (August 29, 1984). RM-4830. *Opposition of Telepictures Corporation to the petition for rulemaking.*

Filmation lets go over 400 staffers in biggest layoff. (December 2, 1987). *Variety,* 44.

Filmation posts lotsa sales action on 'He-Man.' (April 23, 1986). *Variety,* 44.

Fitzgerald, K. (February 3, 1992). Mattel polishes its star power. *Advertising Age,* 10.

Foisie, G. (May 10, 1993). The private profit of public television. *Broadcasting and Cable,* 32.

Forkan, J. (July 9, 1973). Barter series are strong, but not in prime time slots. *Advertising Age,* 3.

Forkan, J. (July 1, 1974). Battle for the 'Apes' set as marketers plan tie-ins. *Advertising Age,* 60.

Forkan, J. (March 1, 1982). Toy products inspired by TV battle military for popularity. *Advertising Age,* 14.

Forkan, J. (April 16, 1984). Children's books pencil in new tie-ins. *Advertising Age,* 64.

Forkan, J. (March 4, 1985). TV toy licensing picking up speed. *Advertising Age,* 38.

Forkan, J. (January 16, 1986). Toy companies' link with TV grows. *Advertising Age,* 38.

Formanek-Brunell, M. (Spring 1993). Marketing a Campbell kids culture. *civitas–Cultural Studies at MIT,* 2(3), 1–5.

Frankel, G. S. (April 9, 1986). Africans enthralled by TV. *The Washington Post,* 1.

Frazier Gross & Kadlec Inc. (January 1986). *Independent thinking: An overview of the independent industry.* Report prepared for the Association of Independent Television.

Freeman, M. (December 20, 1993). Haim Saban: The 'Power' is his. *Broadcasting and Cable,* 26, 30–31.

Freeman, M. (January 3, 1994). Zodiac exits first-run production. *Broadcasting and Cable,* 45, 65.

Frisbie O'Donnell, F. (March 1933). Every child needs an allowance. *Parents' Magazine,* 18, 19, 38, 40.

Gelman, M. (February 2, 1984). 'He-Man' leads way for first run fare. *Electronic Media,* 34–35.

Gilbert, E. (1957). *Advertising and marketing to young people.* Pleasantville, NY: Printer's Ink Books.

Ginsberg, M. (January 1991). Animated features back on the drawing board. *The Hollywood Reporter,* S12–13, S44–45.

Global ads for kids stymie Parker Bros. (June 25, 1984). *Variety,* 72.

Goerne, C. (November 9, 1992). Nick's rude 'Ren & Stimpy' hits it big with licensed goods. *Marketing News,* 26, 2, 6.

Golding, P., & Murdock, G. (1979). Ideology and the mass media: The question of determination. In M. Barrett (Ed.), *Ideology and cultural production.* New York: St. Martin's Press.

Goldman, K. (November 13, 1985). Sponsors call the shots on public tv. *Variety,* 93.

Greenberg, J. (March 1, 1985). Moppet market still viable in U.S., many distribs miss out. *Variety,* 1.

Greene, R., & Spragins, E. (November 8, 1982). Smurfy to the max. *Forbes,* 67–70.

Grillo, J. (January 1988). The cautious survivors. *Channels,* 64–65.

Grossman, G. (1980). *Saturday morning T.V.* New York: Delacourt Press.

Group W, Mattel Toys team for TV. (December 20, 1982). *Advertising Age,* 20.

Group W readies made-for-syndie animation series. (December 15, 1982). *Variety,* 53.

Groves, D. (July 11–17, 1994). 'Lion' king of o'seas box office. *Variety,* 14.

Gruenberg, B., & Gruenberg, S. (December 1931). Teaching children the use of money. *Parents' Magazine,* 48(6), 22–24, 48–50.

Gruenberg, S. M. (December 1934). The dollar sign in family life. *Parents' Magazine,* 18.

Gruenburg, S. M., & Grueberg, B. (1933). *Parents, children, and money.* New York: Viking Press.

Grumbine, E. E. (March 1935a). Age groups of children: Part I. *Printer's Ink Monthly,* 28–30, 48.

Grumbine, E. E. (April 1935b). Age groups of children: Part II. *Printer's Ink Monthly,* 34–36, 38, 70–72.

Grumbine, E. E. (1938). *Reaching juvenile markets.* New York: McGraw-Hill.

Guber, S. (December 23, 1985). Children as consumers. *Advertising Age,* 12.

Guider, E. (April 26, 1989). Disney, Scottish tv team to coproduce kids' series to air on Brit network. *Variety,* 6.

Hanna–Barbera's TV folks bring cheer to licensees. (February 16, 1976). *Advertising Age,* 58.

Harmetz, A. (September 30, 1985). 'Kid vid,' a growing segment of cassette market. *The New York Times.*

Harrington, R. (February 18, 1990). New toys on the block. *The Washington Post,* F1.

Hasbro's urge to merge: Quality first. (March 1985). *Chain Store Age, General Merchandise Trends,* 84.

Helitzer, M., & Heyel, C. (1970). *The youth market: Its dimensions, influence, and opportunities for you.* New York: Media Books.

Hinckley, D. (December 27, 1991). Stars' songs for kids no longer small fry. *The Miami Herald,* 6E.

Holland, P. (1992). *What is a child?* London: Virago Press.

Hollander, S. C., & Germain, R. (1992). *Was there a Pepsi generation before Pepsi discovered it?* Lincolnwood, IL: NTC Business Books.

Home VCR study: Kids lead adults by almost double. (June 22, 1988). *Variety,* 1.

Hot Wheels doesn't push Mattel toys; Mattel pushes 'Hot Wheels' toys, FCC says. (February 16, 1970). *Advertising Age,* 3, 46.

How they keep the Smurfs under control. (December 5, 1983). *Sales and Market Management,* 63–64.

Hoynes, W. (1994). *Public television for sale: Media, the market, and the public sphere.* Boulder, CO: Westview Press.

Indie specialists weigh success, majors' impact, product glut, quality 'gap' . . . (August 13, 1991). *Billboard,* C3, C8–9, C14.

Indies get sizable shares in access see it with double vision—separately and part of whole. (January 30, 1978). *Television/Radio Age,* 67.

Jeffrey, D. (February 13, 1993). Playing ball on Disney's field. *Billboard,* C4.

Jensen, E. (January 13, 1994). Public TV prepares for image transplant to justify existence. *The Wall Street Journal,* 1.

Jereski, L. (September 1983). Advertisers woo kids with a different game. *Marketing Media Decisions,* 72–73, 126–128.

Jolson-Colburn, J. (January 23, 1996). DIC, Rhino join for kiddie label. *The Hollywood Reporter,* 4, 197.

Katz, J. (July 9, 1994). Go, go, Power Rangers! *TV Guide,* 6–16.

Kerkman, D., Kunkel, D., Huston, A., Wright, J., & Pinon, M. (Spring 1990). Children's television programming and the 'free market solution.' *Journalism Quarterly, 67*(1), 147–156.

Kesler, L. (June 1, 1987). Wider market awareness a tempting enticement. *Advertising Age,* S2.

Kideo video to debut with seven cassettes for issue this month. (November 6, 1985). *Variety,* 83.

Kid's records spinning off. (April 16, 1984). *Advertising Age,* 64.

Kids web finds Latin sandbox. (September 16–22, 1996). *Variety,* 29, 47.

KidVid forces link to attack market. (August 19, 1987). *Variety,* 47.

KidVid going international, coproduction deals form many new partnerships. (April 27, 1988). *Variety,* 114.

Kidvideo chart review. (October 5, 1985). *Billboard,* CE10.

Kilburn, D. (October 7, 1991). Japan TV surge to hike need for foreign shows. *Advertising Age,* 114.

Kinder, M. (1991). *Playing with power in movies, television, and video games: From Muppet Babies to Teenage Mutant Ninja Turtles.* Berkeley: University of California Press.

Kline, S. (1993). *Out of the garden: Toys, TV, and children's culture in the age of marketing.* London: Verso.

Kunkel, D., & Roberts, D. (1991). Young minds and marketplace values: Issues in children's television advertising. *Journal of Social Issues, 47*(1), 57–72.

Laybourne, G. (1993). The Nickelodeon experience. In G. L. Berry & J. K. Asamen (Eds.), *Children and television.* Newbury Park, CA: Sage.

Leisure Concepts, Inc. (1986a). *10K report.* New York: Author.

Leisure Concepts, Inc. (1986b). *10K report.* New York: Author.

Leisure Concepts marks record quarter, half. (August 19, 1987). *Variety,* 3, 38.

Levin, G. (April 8–14, 1996). Disney, Mattel ink three-year deal. *Variety.*

Licensing deal signed by PBS. (April 28, 1995). *The New York Times,* C4.

Licensing letter. (1991). Scottsdale, AZ: Arnold Bolka.

Liebeck, L. (June 6, 1994). Licensing is not mere child's play. *Discount Store News, 19,* 45.

'Lion' vid wows with huge sales numbers. (March 13–19, 1995). *Variety,* 26.

Litman, B. (1979). *The vertical structure of the television broadcasting industry: The coalescence of power.* East Lansing, MI: Division of Research, Graduate School of Business Administration, Michigan State University.

Loftus, J. (June 30, 1982). 'Smurfs' power NBC kidvid sales surge. *Variety,* 37, 44.

Loftus, J. (November 9, 1987). U.S. distributors climbing aboard merchandise wagon. *Television/Radio Age,* 63–64.

Lor-Tel woos kidvid buyers with p'time pic. (June 11, 1986). *Variety,* 46, 53.

Lorimar/Telepictures. (1985). *Barter syndication: A white paper.* Report prepared by Telepictures Corporation.

Luke, C. (1990). *Constructing the child viewer: A history of the American discourse on television and children, 1950–1980.* New York: Praeger.

MacGregor, M. (1984). *The ignominious death of FCC docket 19142: Ending the crusade for children's television.* Association for Education in Journalism and Mass Communication, University of Florida, Gainesville, Florida.

Masters' premiere held in grand Hollywood style. (December 1983). *Playthings,* 62.

Mattel, Inc. (1984). *Annual report.* El Segundo, CA: Author.

Mattel, Inc. (1986). *Annual report.* El Segundo, CA: Author.

Mattel, Inc. (1992). *Annual report.* El Segundo, CA: Author.

Mattel Toys debuts tv syndication arm. (November 29, 1986). *Variety,* 144.

Mattel's Handlers on the super future. (September 1970). *Playthings,* 56–57.

Mayer, I. (epm Communications). (October 6, 1992). [Letter to Norma Pecora]. Brooklyn, New York.

Mayer, R., Zussman, J., & Stamp R., II. (1979). Consumer socialization of children. *International Consumer, 19*(2), 12–22.

McClellan, S. (July 6, 1992). Twinkle set for syndication. *Broadcasting,* 34.

McClorey, B. (October 1984). Europe maps out licensing activity. *Playthings,* 84–85.

McCormick, M. (February 8, 1992a). Show & sell—and other tips on moving music. *Billboard,* 70.

McCormick, M. (December 25, 1992b). Kid biz grew up as majors stood up and took notice. *Billboard,* 67–68.

McCormick, M. (August 28, 1993a). Kids' audio. *Billboard,* H20, H22, H24, H26–H27.

McCormick, M. (December 25, 1993b). Kids' music enters that awkward stage. *Billboard,* 78.

McCormick, M. (February 19, 1994a). The ABCs of audio. *Billboard,* 68, 81–82.

McCormick, M. (August 27, 1994b). Children's audio. *Billboard,* 84–85, 90–91, 93–94, 96.

McCormick, M. (July 1, 1995). Preschool video comes of age. *Billboard,* 95–100.

McGann, A., & Russell, J. T. (1981). *Advertising media: A managerial approach.* Homewood, IL: Richard D. Irwin.

McNeal, J. (1987). *Children as consumers: Insights and implications.* Lexington, MA: D. C. Heath.

McNeal, J. (1992). *Kids as customers.* New York: Lexington Books.

Mehegan, D. (December 2, 1990). A cure for toy troubles. *Boston Globe,* 93.

Melanson, J. (March 6, 1985a). Vid deals for '85 toy characters surface following Gotham Fair. *Variety,* 340.

Melanson, J. (November 20, 1985b). Random House, CTW cement 'Sesame Street' HV contract; first tapes due out mid-1986. *Variety,* 99.

Melody, W. (1973). *Children's television: The economics of exploitation.* New Haven, CT: Yale University Press.

Melody, W., & Ehrlich, W. (August 1976). Children's TV commercials: The vanishing policy options. *Journal of Communication, 24*(4), 113–125.

Meyrowitz, J. (1985). *No sense of place.* New York: Oxford University Press.

Mickey and Bambi meet Mandy and Billy. (November 19, 1992). *The New York Times,* C3.

Miller, A. (Summer/Fall 1990). Work and what it's worth. *Newsweek Special Issue, 65*(27), 28–29, 30, 33.

Moppet aud is latest target of video programmers. (August 10, 1983). *Variety,* 39.

Move over Snoopy—A Belgian gnome is Smurfing up the kiddie market. (September 27, 1982). *People Weekly,* 45–46.

Murdock, G., & Golding, P. (1974). For a political economy of mass communication. In R. Miliband & J. Saville (Eds.), *The Socialist Register, 1973.* London: Merlin Press.

Mutter, J. (1995). Books wherever you look. *Publisher's Weekly Outlook,* 23–25.

Nashawaty, C. (June 10, 1994). Card Blanche. *Entertainment Weekly,* 74.

NBC fumbles in cabbage patch. (December 17, 1983). *TV Guide,* A1.

NBC Merchandising Division. (1932). *The NBC handbook on offers and contests.* New York: National Broadcasting Company, Inc.

NBC Statistical Department. (April 1932). *A study of the network broadcast advertising of the food industry.* New York: National Broadcasting Company, Inc.

Neff, M. L. (August 1994). *Defining 'educational or informational' children's television programming.* Association for Education in Journalism and Mass Communication, Qualitative Studies Division.

Newcomb, P. (June 11, 1990). Hey dude, let's consume. *Forbes,* 126–131.

Nichols, P. M. (January 16, 1995). Home video: Sony branches out by licensing children's video. *The New York Times,* B6.

Nickelodeon's corporate past: Nickelodeon/Nick at Nite chronology. (April 5–11, 1989). *Variety,* 70.

No miscues in 'Hot Wheels' deal, ABC, NAB reassures FCC. (December 22, 1969). *Advertising Age,* 1.

Now Billy, age 6 picks brands. (March 1983). *Marketing and Media Decisions,* 68–69.

O'Connor, K. (February 13, 1993). They believe that children are the future. *Billboard,* C3.

Owen, D. (October 1986). Where toys come from. *Atlantic Monthly,* 65.

Pagano, P. (June 6, 1984). Ban asked on kidvid profit plan. *Los Angeles Times,* VI1.

Parker Bros. bows kidisk line with Cabbage Patch LP. (February 15, 1984). *Variety,* 102.

Pecora, N. (August 1991). *Local children's television or 'Whatever happened to Captain Bob?'* Association for Education in Journalism and Mass Communication, Boston, Massachusetts.

Pecora, N. (May 1993). *The environment of children's advertising.* International Communication Association, Washington, DC.

Pecora, N. (1994). *TV Guide database*. Unpublished.

Phillips, L. (September 21, 1987). Sony line tunes in kids. *Advertising Age*, 12.

Postman, N. (1985). *Amusing ourselves to death*. New York: Penguin Books.

Prism's Marvel library reduces January titles to 6 from original 12. (November 13, 1985). *Variety*, 41.

Promo tie-ins for Chipmunk's feature. (March 25, 1987). *Variety*, 7.

Public TV attracts upscale sponsors. (April 18, 1994). *Broadcasting and Cable*, 39.

Really 'Bogus.' (November 19, 1990). *Broadcasting*, 30.

Reeves, B., & Baughman, J. (1983). Fraught with such great possibilities: The historical relationship of communication research to mass media regulation. In O. Gandy, P. Espinosa, & J. Ordover (Eds.), *Proceedings from the 10th Annual Telecommunications Policy Research Conference*. Norwood, NJ: Ablex.

Reisman, D., Glasser, N., & Revel, D. (1979). The mass media in the stage of other direction: The child market. In G. Gumpert & R. Cathcart (Eds.), *Intermedia*. New York: Oxford University Press.

Revolution under way in TV programming. (June 1985). New York: Standard & Poor Corp.

Reysen, F. (August 1982). Retailers exploit licensing boom. *Playthings*, 36–38, 40, 84.

Roman, M. (January 23, 1996). Licensed goods bring in $70 bil. *The Hollywood Reporter*, 8, 193.

Rosenfeld, M. (November 29, 1992). Tie-in marketers refuse to leave us home alone. *Boston Globe*, A6.

Rowland, W. (1983). *The politics of TV violence*. Beverly Hills, CA: Sage.

Rowland, W., & Tracey, M. (May 27, 1993). *Lessons from abroad: A preliminary report on the condition of public broadcasting in the United States and elsewhere*. Paper presented to a joint meeting of the International Communication Association and the American Forum of the American University, Washington, DC.

Sales growth slowed sharply in '85. (February 1986). (Standard & Poor's Industry Survey). New York: Standard & Poor Corp.

Schine, E., & McWilliams, G. (February 17, 1992). Mattel: Looking for a few good boy toys. *Business Weekly*, 116, 118.

Schneider, C. (1987). *Children's television: The art, the business and how it works*. Lincolnwood, IL: NTC Business Books.

Schulman, M. (February 1992). Licensers focus on the long view. *Playthings*, 144–146, 151–153.

Seiter, E. (1993). *Sold separately: Parents and children in consumer culture.* New Brunswick, NJ: Rutgers University Press.

Seldes, G. (February 1938). Diamond pin money. *Photoplay,* 22–23, 84–85.

Seligman, D. (November 14, 1983). The commercial crisis. *Fortune,* 39.

Sell the kids, sell the parents. (May 31, 1965). *Broadcasting,* 32, 34.

The selling of the Smurfs. (April 5, 1982). *Newsweek,* 56.

Shaffer, H. (August 25, 1965). Youth market. *Editorial Research Reports,* 623–641.

Shelby, M. (Summer 1964). Children's programming trends on network television. *Journal of Broadcasting,* 8, 247–256.

Shister, G. (May 20, 1991). Ghostwriter. *Boston Globe,* 50.

Short, W. H. (1928). *A generation of motion pictures.* New York: Garland Publishing. (Reprinted 1978, Arno Press)

Siemicki, M., Atkin, D., Greenberg, B., & Baldwin, T. (Winter 1986). Nationally distributed children's shows: What cable TV contributes. *Journalism Quarterly,* 63(4), 710–718.

Simmons Market Research Bureau, Inc. (1991). *The Kids Study.* New York: Author.

Smurfs now bartered for '86; only Taft stations get first dibs. (March 21, 1984). *Variety,*

Smurfun [The official newsletter of the Smurf Fun Club]. (1983). Woodland Hills, CA.

Sobel, R. (November 21, 1983). Daytime television to undergo new challenges; value of barter is being questioned by stations. *Television/Radio Age,* 104–106, 252.

Sobel, R. (February 6, 1984a). Games, 'cash-plus' up; off network is down. *Television/Radio Age,* 141–147, 338–342.

Sobel, R. (October 14, 1985). Proposed Lorimar, Telepictures deal joins 2 strong firms. *Television/Radio Age,*

Sports Illustrated launches magazine for kids. (March 27, 1989). *Marketing News,* 6.

Sterling, C. H., & Kittross, J. M. (1990). *Stay tuned: A concise history of American broadcasting.* Belmont, CA: Wadsworth.

Stern, S. (October 5, 1987). Youth movement: Fisher–Price turns on kid video. *Advertising Age,* 90.

Stern, S., & Schoenhaus, T. (1990). *Toyland: The high stakes game of the toy industry.* Chicago: Contemporary Books.

Stevenson, W. (June 1, 1992). Studios marching to the beat of toons. *Variety,* 49.

Stipp, H. (February 1988). Children as consumers. *American Demographics*, 27–32.

Stipp, H. (August 1993). New ways to reach children. *American Demographics*, 50–51, 54, 56.

Strasser, S. (1989). *Satisfaction guaranteed.* New York: Pantheon Books.

Syndicators unleash flood of first-run kid product. (August 20, 1984). *Television/Radio Age*, 33–37, 80–81, 84.

Summers, H. (1971). *A thirty year history of programs carried on national radio networks in the United States, 1926–1956.* New York: Arno Press.

Taking a second look at barter. (December 21, 1992). *Broadcasting*, 4, 10.

Telepictures to pitch first-run cartoon series. (June 13, 1984). *Variety*, 41.

Telerep arm gets U.S. syndie rights to 'Smurf' series. (January 18, 1984). *Variety*, 54.

Thorburn, A. L. (1990). Regulating television for the sake of children. *University of Detroit Law Review*, 67(3), 413–441.

Tip-Top Trolls. (January 9, 1992). *The London Sun*, Mega Guide, 1.

Tobenkin, D. (June 13, 1994). Walking the kids tightrope. *Broadcasting and Cable*, 19.

Tonka to acquire Kenner Parker. (September 5, 1987). *Washington Post*, D10.

Top kid videos. (January 9, 1993). *Billboard*,

Top 100 markets: Mattel. (September 26, 1985). *Advertising Age*, 100.

Top 100 markets: Mattel. (September 4, 1986). *Advertising Age*, 106.

Toys and television: Paying partnership. (May 28, 1956). *Broadcasting–Telecasting*, 48.

Toys 'R' Us announces plan to build 115 stores in 1994. (January 12, 1994). *The New York Times*.

Trachtenberg, J. (November 3, 1986). Big spenders: Teenage division. *Forbes*, 201.

Tribune, Telerep conclude pact on barter time. (June 17, 1987). *Variety*, 69.

Triplett, T. (September 26, 1994). Ren and Stimpy rub elbows with Barbie. *Marketing News*, 2.

Turow, J. (Summer 1980). Television sponsorship forms and program subject matter. *Journal of Broadcasting*, 24, 381–397.

Turow, J. (1981). *Entertainment, education, and the hard sell.* New York: Praeger.

Two executives promoted by Mattel. (July 24, 1992). *The New York Times,* D2.

U.S. Department of Commerce, National Telecommunications and Information Administration. (January 1993). *Globalization of the mass media.* Washington, DC: U.S. Government Printing Office.

U.S. Department of Commerce. (January 1992). *U.S. industrial outlook '92 (Dolls, toys, games, and children's vehicles)* (pp. 38:6–9). Washington, DC: Author.

Upton, P. (1985). *Make millions in the licensing business.* New York: Monarch Press.

Viacom executives discuss expanding Nickelodeon overseas. (May 1, 1989). *Broadcasting,* 131.

Viacom, Inc. (1992). *Annual report.* New York: Author.

Viacom–Par merger: What's in it. (February 21, 1994). *Variety,* 185.

Walley, W. (January 23, 1995). Syndication as a piece of the puzzle. *Electronic Media,* 12, 20.

Walt Disney Company. (1984). *Annual report.* Burbank, CA: Author.

Walt Disney Company. (1992). *Annual report.* Burbank, CA: Author.

Warner–Amex to charge for MTV, puts spots on Nickelodeon. (March 23, 1983). *Broadcasting,* 34.

Wartella, E., & Pecora, N. (n.d.). *Bibliography of research on children and the media: 1910–1990.* Unpublished.

Wasko, J., Phillips, M., & Purdie, C. (1993). Hollywood meets Madison Avenue: The commercialization of US films. *Media, Culture and Society,* 15, 271–293.

Weisskoff, R. (March 1985). Current trends in children's advertising. *Journal of Advertising Research*

Wildman, S. S., & Siwek, S. E. (1988). *International trade in films and television programs.* Cambridge, MA: Ballinger.

Wilke, J. (March 25, 1985). Are the programs your kids watch simply commercials? *Business Week,* 53–54.

Winn, M. (1984). *Children without childhood.* New York: Penguin Books.

Word on *Widget.* (March 16, 1992). *Broadcasting,* 34.

Year in review: Broadcasting & cable. (1994). *Broadcasting and cable yearbook.* New Providence, NJ: R. R. Bowker.

Youth—the neglected $50 billion market. (July 24, 1964). *Sponsor,* 27–35.

Zelizer, V. (1985). *Pricing the priceless child: The changing social value of children.* New York: Basic Books.

Zimmerman, K. (July 27, 1992). Baby boomers nurture growth in kiddie labels. *Variety,* 64.

Zitner, A. (September 14, 1993). Redstone scripts the future. *Boston Globe,* 37.

Zodiac entertainment enters teen soap derby. (October 30, 1989). *Broadcasting,* 36.

Zodiac to develop animation and teen shows with presales from overseas. (August 21, 1989). *Television/Radio Age,* 45.

Index

Printed in the United Kingdom
by Lightning Source UK Ltd.
107834UKS00001B/19-21